St Benedict and St Thérèse

The Little Rule
&
The Little Way

Other books by Dwight Longenecker

The Path to Rome
Modern Journeys to the Catholic Church

Listen My Son
St. Benedict for Fathers

Adventures in Orthodoxy
*The Marvels of the Christian Creed and
the Audacity of Belief*

and
(with David Gustafson)
Mary: A Catholic-Evangelical Debate

Blessed are you, Father, Lord of heaven and
earth, for revealing the mysteries of the
kingdom to mere children.
— MATTHEW 11:25

St. Benedict and St. Thérèse

The Little Rule & The Little Way

Dwight Longenecker

GRACEWING

Gracewing
2 Southern Avenue, Leominster
Herefordshire HR6 0QF

ISBN 0 85244 521 0

Cover images of St. Benedict and St. Thérèse,
by Brother Claude Lane, O.S.B.; © Mt. Angel Monastery,
all world rights reserved, used with permission
Cover design by Rebecca Heaston
Interior design by Sherri L. Hoffman

For Sister Mary Lucy Reynolds, O.S.C.

Your life is hid with Christ in God.
— COLOSSIANS 3:3

Contents

.

Acknowledgments

The idea for *St. Benedict and St. Thérèse* came during a conference organized by the *Centre for Faith and Culture* at Oxford. Stratford Caldecott, the Director of the Centre, encouraged this work, and I owe him a word of thanks. John Saward spoke at that conference and thought a book drawing Benedict and Thérèse together would be a good idea. Later, he read the manuscript and offered excellent suggestions that helped clarify my thought and expression. Dom Luke Bell, O.S.B., knows far more about both Benedict and Thérèse than I do. He was also good enough to take time to read my manuscript and offer suggestions. His criticisms were clear and precise, and his gentle spirit helped temper my natural stridency. Thanks go to Father John Udris, an expert on St. Thérèse, who also checked the manuscript and made comments. Cyprian Blamires, my colleague at The St. Barnabas Society, read the book and offered helpful suggestions, as did Dom Richard Yeo, O.S.B., the Abbot of Downside.

Thanks also go to David Gustafson and Denise Inge, who both helped with obscure references. I also wish to thank my publishers (or their representatives) — Tom Longford at Gracewing and Mike Dubruiel at Our Sunday Visitor — for their encouragement, patience, and enthusiasm. Editors Jo Ashworth and Henry O'Brien have both been efficient, courteous, and cheerful.

On the personal side, I wish to thank Sister Mary Lucy. O.S.C., for her friendship, prayers, and the example of a hidden life. Dom Sebastian Moore, O.S.B., is an excellent sounding board. He has a sharp mind and a spirit which does "not cease from exploration." I am also grateful to Dom Laurence Kelly,

O.S.B., who always provides profound and practical guidance in my own spiritual journey. I wish to thank the many ordinary priests and people who have encouraged me by expressing their own love for Thérèse and Benedict, and finally I thank my wife, Alison, for her constant support and steadfast love.

— Dwight Longenecker

Introduction

Over twenty years ago while I was studying to be an Anglican minister at an evangelical college in England, a friend in the United States wrote suggesting that I visit a Benedictine monastery. She was a Benedictine oblate herself and she must have sensed in me some sort of religious vocation. For generations my ancestors had been Mennonites — the strictest sort of Anabaptists — and I had been brought up in a devout fundamentalist home in the United States. Becoming an Anglican had been a rather large transition, but the idea of visiting a Catholic monastery was as alien at that time as suggesting that a good Irish Catholic boy might like to drop in on a meeting of the Jehovah's Witnesses.

Nevertheless, I contacted the guestmaster at the closest Benedictine abbey and arranged a visit during my next holiday, which turned out to be during Lent. I arrived with more curiosity than doubt and was immediately captivated by the religious life. Something about the monks caught my imagination. There was the attraction of a centuries-old way of life being followed in the modern world. There was a bookish religious atmosphere that appealed, and I was curious about the details of the monastic experience. More important than this was the opportunity to meet the monks themselves. Even though they wore the same habit, each one seemed far more unique than the monochrome people in the outside world. They were modest and quiet, but there was also a solemn sort of self-mockery about them. Instead of the lugubrious long faces I expected, they projected a certain childlike freedom.

My second visit was on the eve of the Feast of St. Benedict in July. I will never forget a very fat monk saying with eyes aglow,

"You've come at a good time!" Indeed I had. The feast to celebrate St. Benedict's day was replete with smoked salmon, a beautifully cooked main course, followed by strawberries and cream and rounded off with port, chocolates, and a cigar. When I questioned their celebration, they explained about fasts and feasts without the slightest touch of apology or condescension. Coming from a background where both penance and celebration were difficult, it seemed to me that the monks enjoyed a congenial balance of the two.

I began to read the Rule of St. Benedict, and continued to visit monasteries. Five years later, while still an Anglican priest, I had three months free between jobs and decided to hitchhike to Jerusalem from England, staying in Benedictine monasteries en route. As I traveled I got into a routine of walking and prayer, and every night pulled up at a religious community of one sort or another. My journey took me through France and Italy to visit the great Benedictine abbeys of Le Bec, Mont-Saint-Michel, Solesmes, Fleury, Cîteaux, Hautcombe, and Tamie. Crossing the Alps I stopped at Novalesa, Chiaravalle, St. Guistinia, and Camoldoli before going to Monte Oliveto, Subiaco, and Monte Cassino. All along the route the Benedictine spirit was the same: hospitable, dignified and refined yet down to earth, joyful and relaxed. I had thought monks were unusual, perhaps a little eccentric or deranged, certainly religious extremists. Instead there was a naturalness about their religion and life that suddenly made the rest of the world look mad. Here were men who had decided to live together in order to pray, work, and study. They decided to stay in one place and commit themselves to a hard but high quality of life. Their life was vibrant and relevant, yet rooted in venerable and beautiful traditions. We must all give ourselves to something, and their decision seemed far more sensible than chasing money up and down a motorway five days a week.

At the beginning of my journey to Jerusalem I had stopped in the Northern French town of Lisieux simply because I had heard of Thérèse of Lisieux and the map said "pilgrimage center." As an Anglican convert from American fundamentalism I knew next to nothing about St. Thérèse of Lisieux . I'd read snippets about "the little flower" and concluded that the simpering little girl who said a rosary bead every time she went up the stairs was not really to my taste. The first impressions of Lisieux did little to straighten my wrinkled nose. The road up to the ugly basilica was crammed with souvenir shops clattering with dangling rosaries, holy pictures, and lots of Thérèsian tat and papal paraphernalia. Inside the huge church I was turned off by people lighting candles in front of an arm bone of the saint. There was more to come. In the convent church a figure of St. Thérèse lies in a glass coffin surrounded with roses like a prop from a Disney film. Near the convent I went into a darkened side room and saw her hair, her habit, and her writing desk. It seemed all too much like a visit to a wax museum.

I was beginning to be interested in this little saint, but I was still repulsed by a devotion that seemed both alien and tasteless. As an American I thought the French should know better. Nevertheless, I took a room in the Hermitage — a pilgrim's hostel next to the Carmel where the saint had lived and died. That summer evening I went to bed with the window open. I woke up at about three in the morning. The moon was full, and a light breeze was blowing the net curtains at the open window. I was immediately wide awake and aware of a "presence" in my room. The presence seemed to be female and extraordinarily joyful. I am not one for waking dreams and have never had a vision, but I sat up in the bed acutely aware that I was being introduced to something or someone good. I got the impression that the positive presence was that of the saint herself. I sat awake, curious and alert for about a quarter of an hour before the feeling faded and I went back to sleep.

The next morning, remembering my revenant, I visited the bookshop, bought Michael Hollings's biography of St. Thérèse and read it on my journey. I was doubtful about my nighttime experience and put it down to a vivid imagination. However, the experience was disturbing enough to make me remain open-minded about the whole business. As I read the biography, my feelings about Thérèse went from skeptically negative to grudgingly positive. I concluded that, as usual, if so many people thought she was great it must be me who had got it wrong. By the time I got to the end of the book, Thérèse's brilliant spirit had begun to win me over. When I discovered that she prayed for priests, I wondered if I had indeed met her on that summer midnight and stopped to ask if she might pray for me, too, even if I was not a full member of her family.

The trip to Jerusalem was a milestone on my own journey to the Catholic Church. Since being received into full communion, I have found that the lives and writings of Benedict and Thérèse have taken on a new importance for me. One of the main impressions my wife and I had after our reception into the Church was one of intense reality. Like the Catholics I met on my journey, the whole Catholic Church seemed solid and down to earth. Compared with the effete religion that was passed off as "catholic" in the Church of England, the Catholic Church had a humility and reality to it. Newman had expressed the same thing. There was a reality about the Catholic Church that made his former experience seem shallow and unreal. So he wrote in *Difficulties of Anglicans* that "as in fairy tales, the magic castle vanishes when the spell is broken, and nothing is seen but the wild heath, the barren rock, and the forlorn sheepwalk, so it is with us as regards the Church of England, when we look in amazement on what we thought so unearthly and find it so commonplace or worthless."

The reality of the Catholic Church, like all reality, is not always nice. For our family, becoming Catholics meant facing unemployment and the loss of a splendid house and secure career. In England it also meant exchanging the magnificent buildings and high culture of Anglicanism for the brutal buildings, bad music, and drab liturgy of modern English Catholicism. These aesthetic sacrifices have been more than compensated for by a fresh sense of the universality of the Church, and a connection with the Church of the apostles that is more real and vital than I ever could have imagined. There is a down-to-earth quality about Catholicism that, in retrospect, makes Anglicanism seem rather precious and ethereal. This sense of reality makes Catholicism hard, and "hard" means both difficult and concrete.

Benedict and Thérèse are both experts on reality. They teach a spirituality that is down to earth, ordinary, and real. The Benedictine vows of stability, obedience, and conversion of life hammer home the truth that if we cannot find God here and now, we will not be able to find him anywhere. Both Thérèse and Benedict eschew elaborate religion or esoteric spirituality. Their teaching takes us into the heart of the incarnation because they proclaim the constant truth that "God is with us." If God is present in this moment and at this place, then this time and place matter eternally and we had better pay attention because we will never be given a better gate to heaven than this present moment.

Reading books about the Christian life is often a substitute for living it. If it is easy to read spiritual books without being spiritual, it is not much harder to write them without having the experience behind you. Benedict and Thérèse lived before they wrote, and everything they have written was obviously tested by experience. In writing a book about these two saints I hope to point out how their lives and teachings illuminate our experience. In writing about *them* and not about myself I hope to make the point that while they have lived the truth, I have not. Like everyone else, I am on the journey. I only hope that in the reading of this book the lives and writings of this little child and this patriarch might begin to live for others and that they might also be inspired to attempt the little way of Father Benedict and Sister Thérèse.

— DWIGHT LONGENECKER
The Feast of St. Benedict
July 11, 2000

One

The Father
and the Child

Thoughts and Prayers

*"I will arise and go to my father, and I will say to him, 'Father,
I have sinned against heaven and before you.'"*

— LUKE 15:18

*See what love the Father has given us, that we should be called
children of God; and so we are.*

— 1 JOHN 3:1

*Listen, my son, to the instructions of a Master; turn the ear
of your heart to the advice of a loving father.*

— THE RULE OF ST. BENEDICT

*To be little means recognizing one's nothingness, expecting eve-
rything from the good God, as a little child expects everything
from its Father.*

— THÉRÈSE OF LISIEUX

*He who seeks the Father
more than anything He can give
is likely to have what he asks,
for he is not likely to ask amiss.*

— GEORGE MACDONALD

Prayer

*My Father, I abandon myself to you. Do with me as you will.
Whatever you may do with me, I thank you. I am prepared for
anything, I accept everything because you are my Father.*

— CHARLES DE FOUCAULD

C. S. Lewis once observed, "How monotonously alike all the great tyrants and conquerors have been: how gloriously different are the saints."[1] In his little biographies of Thomas Aquinas and St. Francis of Assisi, G. K. Chesterton reveled in the sparkling individuality of both saints. Aquinas was the greatest philosopher of his time, while Francis was a troubadour for Christ. Thomas was a great bull of a man; Francis a scraggy fool of a man. Thomas was a restrained logician; Francis an extravagant poet. In their uniqueness, Aquinas and Francis display the magnificent full-blooded humanity that every saint exhibits.

Chesterton and Lewis weren't the only ones to be delighted by the variety of the saints. Writing to her prioress, Thérèse of Lisieux said, "How different are the variety of ways through which the Lord leads souls!"[2] "Souls are more different than faces."[3] Take three women who share her name: Teresa of Ávila, Teresa Benedicta of the Cross (Edith Stein), and Teresa of Calcutta. They all wear a dull uniform and submit to a regime that seems designed to obliterate their individuality, yet each of them emerges as a feisty, formidable, and utterly unique individual.

The saints are unique because they are ordinary people who have allowed an extraordinary power to bring them to their full potential. The saint is fascinating because she is the person she was created to be; and the more we become who we are, the less we will be like anybody else. The saint has no time for role models. She cannot spend time pretending to be someone else because she realizes it is the work of a lifetime to become oneself.

While the saints are unique, they also complement one another. Threading through the life of every saint is a strand that links them to every other saint. Chesterton shows how Aquinas and Francis, despite their differences, complement each other and reflect the light of Christ back and forth. Thérèse makes a charming observation about how saints depend on one another spiritually. In heaven, she says:

> All the Saints will be indebted to each other. . . . Who knows the joy we shall experience in beholding the glory of the great saints, and knowing that by a secret disposition of Providence we have contributed there unto . . . and do you not think that on their side the great saints, seeing what they owe to quite little souls, will love them with an incomparable love? Delightful and surprising will be the friendships found there — I am sure of it. The favoured companion of an Apostle or a great Doctor of the Church will perhaps be a young shepherd lad; and a simple little child may be the intimate friend of a patriarch.[4]

In the divine drama God creates a cast of heroes and children. The thought is echoed in the words of Pope Pius XI about Thérèse:

> God created such giants of zeal and holiness as Ignatius Loyola and Francis Xavier. Behind these, on the far horizon, we catch a glimpse of Peter and Paul, of Athanasius, Chrysostom, and Ambrose. But behold! The same heavenly Artist has secretly fashioned, with a love well nigh infinite, this maiden so modest, so humble — this child.[5]

Benedict also hints at the surprising complementarity in the communion of saints. For him the magnificent community of heaven is reflected in the monastic community on earth. The monks are not ranked according to social privilege, ability, or age; but in a celestial sort of egalitarianism, they "take their places according to the time of their coming to the monastery, for example, one who has entered the monastery at the second hour is to know that he is junior to him who entered at the first, whatever his age or dignity."[6] As in Thérèse's picture, the young and old respect one another, so Benedict expects the younger monks to show an oriental type of courtesy to their elders: "Whenever the brethren meet one another, the junior should rise and seek a blessing of the elder."[7] However, the older monks should respect the younger because "the youthful Samuel and Daniel acted as judges over their elders,"[8] and in his chapter on summoning the brethren for counsel the older monks must listen respectfully to even the youngest monk, for "it is often to the youngest brother that the Lord reveals the best course."[9]

To study two saints together is to perceive three things: their unique personalities, their similarity to each other, and the way their lives and teachings complement each other. When St. Benedict and St. Thérèse of Lisieux are studied together, the contrast between their personalities is striking. One is an Italian patriarch of the sixth century, the other a bourgeois French girl at the end of the nineteenth. Benedict writes from the edge of the middle age. Thérèse writes from the edge of the modern age. Benedict writes a monastic rule, founds monasteries, rules as an abbot, is visited by royalty, and dies an old man. Like a French Emily Dickinson, Thérèse hardly moves beyond her provincial family circle. She has a pious father, lives an enclosed life, writes poetry and a quaint biography, and dies a painful death at the age of twenty-four. Like Aquinas and Francis, Benedict and Thérèse are radically different personalities; also like Aquinas and Francis, they complement each other in surprising and profound ways. Augustine wrote about the Scriptures that "the New Testament is hidden in the Old and the Old made manifest in the New."[10] So it is with the writings of Thérèse and Benedict; the remarkable insights of Thérèse are hidden within Benedict's simple monastic Rule, and the universal wisdom of Benedict is made fully manifest in the writings of Thérèse. In the two of them Thérèse's picture of the saints in heaven comes true, for in Thérèse and Benedict "a simple little child becomes the intimate friend of a patriarch."

In "studying" a saint, one is never drawn only to the saint's writings. The first attraction to any saint is to that saint's unusual life. The teachings of saints are nothing without their life because their writings and their life are one. As Gregory the Great said of Benedict, "He could not have written what he did not live," and Hans Urs Von Balthasar says, "Thérèse protected herself from ever writing any statement that she herself had not tested and that she was not translating into deeds as she was writing."[11]

Hagiography and biography are not the same thing. We do not study the life of a saint as we might read the story of a dead celebrity. We can't study the story of a dead saint because there's no such thing. The saint's life is dynamic because in Christ the saint is still alive. Thérèse is famous for anticipating the great work she would do after her death. "I will spend my heaven doing good on earth,"[12] she said. We venerate the saints and ask for their intercession not because they have written fine words, nor because we think them especially powerful in heaven. Neither do we venerate the saints and ask for their intercession simply because they are holy and good. We venerate saints and ask for their help because they have become our friends. They may be friends, but they are exalted friends. We relate to the saints as we might to a member of the royal family who has come to call. We are fascinated by them because they are greater than us, but we're more fascinated because they're not greater than us. They might wear satin breeches, but they step into them one leg at a time. Because the saints are like us *and* unlike us they not only show us what we are but what we could be. Studying a saint, therefore, is a work of devotion, not diligence. It is a relationship, not a report. We study a saint not for the love of knowledge but for the knowledge of love.

Certainly Benedict and Thérèse are attractive personalities. Benedict stands as a regal patriarch, calling his followers to a spiritual path of simple moderation. He offers them a civilized and liberating balance of prayer, work, and study. The monasteries that followed his Rule kept the memory of learning alive during a dark age and laid the foundations for modern Western culture. Benedict is a true gentleman of the spirit. He is realistic about human nature but always optimistic about the chances for progress. His personality is cautious and modest yet fervent with brotherly love. Most of all, he is exhilarated by the spiritual life. Disciples of Benedict have been drawn from every corner of the world for over fifteen hundred years. Men and women, religious and laity — all have heard his youthful call to run with him "in the path of God's commandments with hearts overflowing with the inexpressible delight of love."[13]

Thérèse of Lisieux also draws multitudes with her blend of innocence and unrelenting love. She may be "the little flower," but Southerners in the United States would call her a steel magnolia, for her fragrance and purity are undergirded with a determination and resilience like no other. As time turned into the darkest century of human history, Thérèse offered her life and writings as a testimony to the universal values of innocence, faith, and childlike trust. Anyone who perseveres with her writings finds an astounding spiritual depth communicated by a witty and delightful personality. She is tough and tender. She soars with a rhapsody of emotion yet has no time for shallow sentimentality. Anyone who blames her for promoting sugary religion has not read her book to the end.

Benedict of Nursia was born around the year 480 in the Umbrian province of Italy. According to his biography, written by Pope St. Gregory the Great, Benedict was born into a "family of high station." As a young man he went to Rome to study but was disgusted by the decadent life of the city. Some seventy years before Benedict's birth, Rome had fallen to the barbarians. By the middle of the fifth century the Huns were ransacking Northern Italy, and Rome had been pillaged for a second time. By the time Benedict went to Rome to study, at about the turn of the fifth century into the sixth, the old Empire was in tatters. Civilization had crumbled into chaos, and the social disorder was reflected in further conflict within the Church and every institution.

Benedict decided to run away from the city. He headed for Subiaco, a wild region just south of Rome, where he lived in a cave for three years. The site overlooked the ruins of Nero's palace and the remnants of a Roman aqueduct. Looking over the ruins, Benedict must have felt like Shelley's traveler from an antique land who happens across the colossal ruins of the once great and disdainful king Ozymandias. The desert left by the barbarian invasions had spread across the proud Roman Empire, and those of Benedict's generation were left to reflect on the remnants and pick up the pieces. By fleeing civilization Benedict saved it, for it was the monasteries of Benedict that eventually preserved the culture of the ancient world. Someone has said, "In a world of fugitives, the one who runs away may be the only one who is heading home." So Benedict in heading for the hills was heading for home in the highest sense.

Eventually some other monks heard about Benedict's holiness and invited him to be their abbot. His holiness must have been more attractive from a distance, however, because disgruntled with his high standards, some of the monks tried to poison him. Benedict shook the dust from his feet and went back to

Subiaco, where he established twelve small monasteries, each with about twelve monks. Based on that experiment he left Subiaco in about 529 to establish a monastery on the hilltop of Monte Cassino in Central Italy. He lived there for the rest of his life and gained a great reputation as a holy man. At Monte Cassino he drew from earlier monastic authors to compose a new monastic rule. It is a simple set of guidelines for a community life based around a balance of prayer, work, and study. Benedict's Rule is the work of spiritual genius. It has stood the test of time because of Benedict's deep understanding of human nature. The Rule's practical insights are flexible, moderate, and wise. They prepare the ground for a truly simple spirituality to flourish.

Chesterton said, "It is a paradox of history that each generation is converted by the saint who contradicts it most."[14] Benedict lived in an age of extreme action and reaction, decadence, chaos, war, and despair. He saved it by establishing communities based on moderation and communication, chastity, order, peace, and prayer. That his little Rule has lasted for fifteen hundred years only shows how every age cries out for the unchanging ideals that this gentleman of the Spirit provides.

Gregory the Great's biography of Benedict portrays not only a holy man but a wonder worker. Whether or not the miracles in Gregory's life of Benedict happened exactly as related is beside the point. The fact is, the miracles are fun. They are full of didactic entertainment and earthy humor. It is both entertaining and instructive that Benedict thought the blackbirds were demons. Perhaps they were. There is something demonic about blackbirds, and it makes a good story — like something out of Edgar Allen Poe. In the legends there's one soberingly funny story about an enemy of Benedict who sent seven ladies to dance in the monastery garden to tempt the young monks. Later a building fell down and killed the evil man. Of course the saint was sorry for his enemy's death, but it does sound like the time Elisha summoned a bear to maul the lads who mocked his bald-headedness.

It's fun to think the miracles happened, but the main problem is not whether they happened or not, but whether they matter. Certainly Benedict himself would have taken a sanguine attitude to such phenomena. As Teresa of Ávila was annoyed and embarrassed by her levitation, so Benedict would probably have been more concerned about the novices being late for Matins than about making an iron pruning hook float for a Gothic peasant. Benedict would have been unconcerned about difficulties of miracles because he was more concerned with the difficulties of real life. He could have rephrased the Lord's command and said, "Take no thought for miracles; today has enough worries to concern you."

Benedict's concern for the detail of daily life comes through his Rule. There we have his portrait, and the person we meet is a wise, dignified, and loving man. He is thoughtful and compassionate while also being shrewd and strict. The mystic side of his character is shown in his experience one night when praying. Suddenly it seemed to him that "the whole world seemed to be caught up into one sunbeam and gathered thus before his eyes." He died in the monastic chapel where he received communion, and then passed away like Moses, standing erect for battle with his outstretched arms supported by his monks.

The details of Benedict's life and character can only be pieced together with the few documents that remain from his time. With Thérèse the opposite is true. Her work *The Story of a Soul* is an autobiography. As she is such a relatively modern figure we have photographs of her as well as the documents from the canonization process. The nuns she left behind recorded their memories of the saint in detail. Her last surviving sister died as recently as 1959. If Benedict seems remarkable for his heroic life, the story of Thérèse's life is remarkable for its ordinariness. She didn't run from the city to live in a cave and be fed by birds. She went into a convent in her hometown, as many girls of her generation did. Thérèse is a modern saint precisely because she comes from such an ordinary background. She is a saint for Everyman.

Marie Françoise Thérèse Martin was born in Alençon in Normandy on January 2, 1873. Her father was a watchmaker and her mother made lace to supplement the family income. In the summer of 1877 her mother died, and that autumn M. Martin moved his family to a small house called Les Buissonets in the nearby town of Lisieux. In a nice link with St. Benedict, Thérèse was educated by the Benedictine sisters at the convent school in Lisieux.

Thérèse was a sensitive and loving child brought up in a very devout but conventional middle-class home. She had already lost her mother, and by the time she was thirteen two of her older sisters had left the family to enter the Carmelite convent in Lisieux. The Carmelites were an enclosed contemplative order, and when a girl entered the Carmel she took quite literally Christ's call to leave one's family for the sake of the kingdom. The nun would never again leave the convent, and family visits would be rationed and monitored.

By the time Thérèse was fourteen she was determined to follow her sisters into the strict regime of prayer in the Carmel at Lisieux. Rules forbade entrance to the convent at such an early age, but Thérèse persisted, first winning her father's approval, then finally the bishop's, by the winter of 1887. In the meantime, on a visit to Rome she had the nerve to disobey all the adults and ask Pope Leo XIII himself for approval to enter the convent. He is reported to have smiled, patted her cheek, and muttered that if it was God's will she would enter. It was God's will, for in April of 1888, when she was fifteen, Thérèse entered the Carmel of Lisieux and stayed there until her death from tuberculosis some nine years later. It is a beautiful coincidence that she died, like Benedict, with her arms outstretched and supported by her sisters. Her sister Céline recalls the last hours of Thérèse's life: "She was suffering extremely in all her muscles, and placing one arm on Mother Agnes' shoulder and the other on mine, she remained thus — her arms in the form of a cross. At that very moment, three o'clock sounded, and the thought of Jesus on the Cross came to our mind."[15]

Thérèse's life in the convent did not seem extraordinary. The convent's regime was too relaxed for her, and there was no pressure for great deeds of mortification. Her holiness was hidden within this ordinary life, and most people were unaware of her remarkable perfection. Indeed when asked about her later, many of her fellow nuns said there was nothing particularly heroic about Thérèse. One sister summed up the opinion of most of the nuns: "I cannot understand why people speak of Sister Thérèse as if she were a saint. She never does anything notable."[16] Despite her hiddenness, there were some in the convent who recognized the holiness within the humility. Her prioress, Mother Marie de Gonzague, reported of the seventeen-year-old Thérèse, "This angelic child is only seventeen and a half; yet she has the judgement of a woman of thirty, the religious perfection of an old and accomplished novice."[17] Three years later she paints a portrait of an attractive and sparkling personality: "Tall and robust, with a childlike face, and with a tone of voice and expression that hides a wisdom, a perfection and a perspicacity of a woman of fifty. . . . She is a little innocent thing . . . whose head is filled with tricks to be played on anyone she pleases. A mystic, a comedienne, she is everything! She can make you shed tears of devotion and she can as easily make you split your sides with laughter."[18]

Apart from an incident in childhood when a statue of the Virgin Mary seemed to smile and heal her, Thérèse was not surrounded by stupendous events. Nevertheless, like Benedict she was thought to have the ability to "read souls"; she had many amazing answers to prayer, and she experienced a stream of graces that many would think were miraculous. She didn't think so. She steadfastly refused to follow a path of miracles and visions. She writes, "I do not wish to see the good God here on earth. No. Not in the least. And yet I love him. I also love the Mother of God and the saints very much; but I do not wish to see them either. I prefer to live in faith."[19]

If every generation is converted by the saint who contradicts it most, then Thérèse is the saint for our age. In a time of self-indulgent, pseudo-sophisticated individuality, Thérèse is innocent, ordinary, and anonymous. In an age of technological "miracles," Thérèse is unimpressed. She is a child for an age that despises children and an advocate of "doing nothing special" in a generation of human achievement. Thérèse is a nobody in a world where only "somebodies" matter. She answers cynicism with faith, despair with hope, power with weakness, and hatred with charity.

Thérèse was commanded to write the first parts of her little book as a family memoir. The last part was intended as a contribution to her obituary. Only after her death did her sisters consider publication; and when the first two thousand copies were printed, everyone wondered how they would get rid of so many books. Then in the first twelve years after publication forty-seven thousand copies were sold. In 1914 Pope Pius X introduced her cause for beatification and called her "the greatest saint of modern times." Thérèse was beatified by Pius XI in 1923, and in 1925, just twenty-eight years after her death, St. Peter's was crowded with sixty thousand people for the ceremony of canonization celebrated by Pius XI. The fame and honor of this provincial French girl continued. In 1944 she was declared patroness of France along with Joan of Arc; and at the centenary of her death in 1997 she was declared a Doctor of the Church by Pope John Paul II.

Benedict and Thérèse are the apostles of the ordinary. They both teach a way of spirituality that eschews the heroic in favor of the humble. They are also attractive for deeper reasons. Together they stand as complementary icons in the field of dreams. Benedict is usually shown in his black monastic robes. With his cowl over his head, he holds his pastoral staff in one hand and an open book in the other. Sometimes he is shown with his finger to his lips. That gesture along with the raised cowl is a sign of silence, and a pointer to the Truth beyond words. The staff is a symbol that connects him to all pastors, to Moses, and ultimately to that great shepherd of the sheep, Christ himself. The book is Benedict's famous Rule — but the book is also a symbol of all learning and universal wisdom. A raven stands at his feet like a magus's familiar. According to the legends, the blackbirds fed Benedict in the wilderness as they did Elijah. Together the symbols point to a figure more universal than the historical Benedict alone. Benedict stands as the silent mystic. With his long white beard, his staff, book, and bird, Benedict is the prophet, the seer, and the wise old man. Abbot Benedict assumes an almost mythic dimension in the Christian imagination. He is the archetypal mentor and father figure. He is Abraham and Elijah, Merlin, Teresias, and Gandalf.

Thérèse's image also transcends her own personality. In the iconography she is portrayed in her Carmelite robes, arms clasping a crucifix and an armful of roses. The roses are an emblem of her beauty and innocence. As at an old-fashioned Corpus Christi

celebration, she is the universal flower girl, strewing roses on the
way. She might be a princess from a fairy tale, Snow White or
Rose Red — offering her home and herself to save the suffering
bear. The roses are also an ancient link with the Virgin Mary.
Thérèse's innocence echoes hers. Roses are always a paradoxical
sign. Their thorns are a reminder that their fresh beauty has a
sharp price. As the Virgin of Nazareth suffers with her Son, so
the virgin of Lisieux holds the crucifix like a red badge of courage, for it links her own suffering to the universal suffering of
the cross.

Like Benedict, Thérèse is an archetype. He is the father;
she is the child. In the martyrology he is an ancient Polycarp
facing the flames, she an innocent Lucy embracing the sword.
In the myth, Benedict is the wise old man, Thérèse the innocent
victim. In the fairy story he is the wizard; she is the princess. He
incarnates the wisdom of experience, she the wisdom of innocence. If Benedict is the wise old mentor, Thérèse stands for the
mythic child and the possibility of innocence within each person. She is Eve and Esther, Daphne, Joan of Arc, and Lucy out
of Narnia.

Thérèse and Benedict are powerful figures in the religious
imagination. The old father and the young child connect with
humanity's deepest hopes and dreams. The solid tapestry of adulthood is woven from the dreamlike threads of childhood. Our
daily lives are rooted deeply, and our daily experiences are drawn
from the deepest reservoirs of collective family life. The vices
and virtues of our parents are dynamic in our daily routine. We
are given access to these caverns of the soul through the rites
and relationships of religion. By connecting with Thérèse the
Child and Benedict the Father we make connections to our own
infancy and ancestry. Connecting with Thérèse and Benedict
can bring to the light dark corners of a disturbed childhood and

family history. In praying with them a transaction is agreed. They open the unlocked doors to the depths of our personality we didn't know existed.

The way in is to study, then try to live the simple way of Thérèse and Benedict. As we do, Thérèse and Benedict affect us on a subconscious level. J.R.R. Tolkien helped C. S. Lewis come to faith by saying that the Christian myth "is a true myth, working on us in the same way as the others, but with this tremendous difference that it really happened.' "[20] This is the mystery of the incarnation welling up within the lives of the saints. As the story of Jesus Christ fulfills and completes all the myths and stories that are ever told about dying and rising heroes, so the real lives of the saints help fulfill the truths only partially expressed by the great redemptive stories. St. Paul said in that strangely disturbing phrase that he longed to "fulfil in his sufferings all that was lacking in the cross of Christ."[21] So the saints, like priestly victims, are still bringing the power of sacrifice into the present moment. The dynamic truth about the Christian religion is that the heroic transformations take place in real lives. As the abstract Truth became flesh and dwelt among us in the incarnation, so the truths that the saints teach in their literature are dramatically played out in their lives. As Jesus Christ is the Gospel, so Thérèse and Benedict are the little way. By entering into their lives we enter into their way, and once in their way we may come to share in their heroic transformation.

As founder of Western monasticism, patron of Europe, Doctor of the Church, and patroness of France, Benedict and Thérèse stand as monumental figures in the history of Western society. They can be studied from many perspectives, but they are best studied as father and daughter. In his Rule Benedict speaks to his monks as a loving father. In contrast,

Thérèse writes as a child describing her little way as "the way of spiritual childhood." This complementary perspective sweeps us into the heart of ordinary life, for everyone is a parent or a child or both. Benedict shows us what it means to be a father in relationship with a child. Thérèse shows us what it means to be a child in relationship with a father. Considering Benedict and Thérèse as father and child takes us beyond personal experience into a more profound relationship with God our Father, and as we enter into that experience more fully we come to the very heart of the Godhead, for there Father, Son, and Holy Spirit exist in an eternal relationship of paternal and filial love.

This may sound mighty and metaphysical, but that is the little rock over which people stumble. The ascent to God from the rock of ordinary life is actually at the core of both Benedict and Thérèse's teaching. That's why both saints don't worry too much about miracles. Both saints believe miracles are fancy dress while love wears working clothes. They think anyone can penetrate to the heart of God's love through the reality of everyday life. Because incarnation is the heartbeat of Christianity, Love and Truth are always actions.

Therefore, as long as time shall last, the faithful find God's love locked in ordinary life. With her "little way" Thérèse liberated the faithful from impossible demands of mysticism and asceticism. Her "little way" of love is hidden in Benedict's Rule as well. As Christ came down to earth so Benedict and Thérèse are down-to-earth. Both saints insist that God's love is hidden in all that seems routine and commonplace. Because of this, both Thérèse and Benedict would embrace the hard and simple words of the poet Henry Vaughan: "And here in dust and dirt, O here, / The lilies of His love appear!"[22]

Chapter One Endnotes

1. C. S. Lewis, *Mere Christianity*, London, HarperCollins, 1995, p. 188.

2. Ronald Knox (tr.), *Autobiography of a Saint*, London, Collins, 1973, p. 226.

3. John Clarke, O.C.D. (tr.), *The Story of a Soul: The Autobiography of St. Thérèse of Lisieux*, Washington, D.C., ICS Publications, 1976, p. 277.

4. Thomas N. Taylor (tr.), *Saint Thérèse of Lisieux, The Little Flower of Jesus*, New York, P. J. Kenedy, 1926, p. 302.

5. From a speech at the approval of the miracles attributed to Thérèse's intercessions. Quoted in John Clarke, O.C.D. (tr.), *St. Thérèse of Lisieux: Her Last Conversations*, Washington, D.C., ICS Publications, 1977, p. 5.

6. Abbot Parry (tr.), *The Rule of St. Benedict*, Leominster, Gracewing, 1997, p. 101.

7. Ibid., p. 102.

8. Ibid., p. 101.

9. Ibid., p. 15.

10. Quoted in John Saward, *The Way of the Lamb*, Edinburgh, T&T Clark, 1999, p. 124.

11. Hans Urs Von Balthasar, *Two Sisters in the Spirit*, San Francisco, Ignatius Press, 1970, p. 44.

12. John Clarke, O.C.D. (tr.), *St. Thérèse of Lisieux: Her Last Conversations*, Washington, D.C., ICS Publications, 1977, p. 102.

13. Parry, p. 4.

14. G. K. Chesterton, *St. Thomas Aquinas*, London, Hodder and Stoughton, 1943, p. 17.

15. Clarke, *[St. Thérèse's] Last Conversations*, p. 229.

16. I. F. Görres, *The Hidden Face: A Study of St. Thérèse of Lisieux*, New York, Pantheon, 1959, p. 306.

17. Quoted in Clarke, *[St. Thérèse's] Last Conversations*, p. 16.

18. Ibid.

19. Ibid., p. 188.

20. Quoted in Walter Hooper and Roger Lancelyn Green, *C. S. Lewis — A Biography*, London, Collins, 1974, p. 118.

21. Colossians 1:24.

22. Henry Vaughan, "The Revival," in *The Faber Book of Religious Verse*, ed. Helen Gardner, London, Faber and Faber, 1972, p. 182.

Two

The Little Way
and the Little Rule

Thoughts and Prayers

*Trust in the L*ORD *with all your heart, / and do not rely on your own insight. / In all your ways acknowledge him, / and he will make straight your paths.*

— Proverbs 3:5-6

Enter by the narrow gate; for the gate is wide and the way is easy, that leads to destruction, and those who enter by it are many. For the gate is narrow and the way is hard, that leads to life, and those who find it are few.

— Matthew 7:13-14

The little way is the way of spiritual childhood: the way of trust and of entire self-surrender.

— Thérèse of Lisieux

Whoever you are then, hurrying forward to your heavenly fatherland, do you with Christ's help fulfil this little Rule written for beginners.

— The Rule of St. Benedict

Everywhere the great enters the little —
its power to do so is almost the test of its greatness.

— C. S. Lewis

Prayer
I asked for strength that I might achieve,
I was made weak that I might learn humbly to obey.
I asked for power that I might have the praise of men,
I was given weakness that I might feel my need of God.

— An anonymous Confederate soldier

In his final chapter Benedict says his Rule is "a little Rule for beginners."[1] At first this sounds like the false modesty of the great man of letters. "You have written a masterpiece!" says the fawning devotee. With a superior wave of the hand the guru says, "It is nothing. A few scribblings, a little Rule for beginners, that is all." In one sniff he has elevated himself and relegated his readers to mere beginners. If his attitude were so self-righteous, then he has made an accurate assessment of his book. It is indeed nothing. But Benedict's Rule is *not* "nothing," and he could never be accused of such spiritual pride. Everything else in his writings, his life, and his reputation belies such an interpretation. Perhaps then, when he calls his masterpiece "a little Rule for beginners," he is simply being modest. He knows that much of his Rule is not original. Scholars inform us that the Rule draws heavily on earlier monastic rules. Most of the epilogue is a kind of "further reading" list in which Benedict recommends first the Scriptures, then the writings of the Church Fathers. If his readers really want to be perfect, he urges them to read the other monastic classics of the time: the *Conferences* and *Institutes* that Cassian had collected during his time with the Desert Fathers, the lives of the Fathers, and the Rule of Basil, the founder of Eastern monasticism.

It is true that Benedict is modest about his Rule, but Benedict is a bit like those film heroes who squint and don't say much. When he does say something, it is loaded with meaning. After he calls his Rule "a little Rule for beginners," Benedict assures his monks that if they follow the Rule they will "come at the end, under God's protection, to those heights of learning and virtue mentioned above."[2] In other words, although Benedict calls his Rule "a little Rule for beginners," he realizes that his way is enough to bring the spiritual seeker to perfection.

Benedict thinks perfection is achieved through discipline,

prayer, and action. In the Prologue he rallies his sons in the faith: "Let us make a girdle for ourselves out of faith and perseverance in good works . . . for if we wish to make our home in the dwelling place of his kingdom there will be no getting there unless we run towards it by good deeds."[3] In other words, practice makes perfect. Heaven is for the long-distance runner, not the sprinter. At the end of the Prologue he echoes the Gospel, which says that those who persevere to the end will be saved. Benedict says, "Let us then never withdraw from discipleship to him, but persevering in his teachings in the monastery till death, let us share the suffering of Christ through patience, and so deserve also to share in his kingdom."[4]

Benedict's "little Rule" is a way of discipline, sacrifice, and good works, but no one should make the mistake of thinking Benedict teaches salvation by works. Benedict doesn't expect his sons to be spiritual supermen. In the Prologue he says he wants to "establish a school for the Lord's service, and in setting it up we hope we shall lay down nothing that is harsh or hard to bear."[5] This is not because Benedict is soft. Not only does he realize that excessive whipcracking is counter-productive, but he knows nobody gets into heaven by good works anyway. He doesn't quote the particular verse, but he knows that passage which thunders from the Reformers: "For by grace you have been saved through faith; . . . it is the gift of God — not because of works, lest any man should boast."[6]

In the Prologue Benedict roots the whole monastic enterprise in God's grace. He begins by setting up the ground rules: "First of all, whenever you begin any good work, you must ask of God with the most urgent prayer that it may be brought to completion by him."[7] This principle is fleshed out with Benedict's later instruction that each office must begin with the ancient prayer "O God, come to my assistance; O Lord, make haste to help me."[8] The monk must follow the famous dictum of St. Augustine, "Pray as if everything depends on God; work as if everything depends on you."

In the middle of the Prologue Benedict explains what the perfect Christian looks like. His list reads like a second Sermon on the Mount. It is Benedict's Beatitudes. The blessed person is:

> He who walks without fault and does what is right; he who tells the truth in his heart; he who works no deceit with his tongue; he who does no wrong to his neighbour; he who does not slander his neighbour. He who casts the wicked devil, even as he beguiles him, out of the sight of his heart, along with the temptation itself.[9]

But these good works aren't enough. Benedict crowns the list with an inner gift without which the other virtues are mere virtue. The perfect disciple "does not become conceited about keeping the law well, but realizes that the good in himself cannot be his own work but is done by the Lord, and who praises the Lord working within him."[10] The monk who has virtue without grace is a sort of spiritual parvenu. He is like the schoolboy musician who practices hard but has no talent; everyone admires his worthiness but not his music. There is simply no room in Benedict's community for someone who is trying to climb his way into heaven. Benedict's disciple must constantly look to God for help. He looks to God because God is looking at him. Throughout the Rule Benedict reminds his monks that God is watching, and that they live in the presence of God, the saints, and the holy angels. God is present as a judge, but not as some celestial Scrooge. Instead God the Father is present as a wise mentor — looking over their shoulder to help them with their lessons. His discipline is always correction, not punishment. Benedict's reliance on grace is most clearly stated in the final call to arms in the Prologue: "We must make ready our hearts and bodies to engage in the warfare of holy obedience to Christ's commands, and because our nature has not power to do this, we must ask God to send forth the help of his grace to our aid."[11]

Protestants have often raised the guy of Pelagianism, accusing Catholics of keeping alive that old heresy, salvation by works. Monks and nuns especially were accused of trying to earn their salvation. Like all guys this is a straw man. It was the Catholic Church in the early fifth century that first condemned the notion that anyone could earn heaven. The heresy had almost died out by the sixth century, but Semi-Pelagianism, a kind of ghost of Pelagianism, was still haunting the Church in Benedict's lifetime. Benedict, along with the other orthodox teachers of the time, exorcises the ghost with his stout and constant reliance on grace. Benedict's little daughter Thérèse also says "boo" to modern Semi-Pelagian spooks. In a statement worthy of Luther she says, "In the evening of this life I shall appear before you empty-handed, for I do not ask you, Lord, to count my works. All our justices have stains in your sight. So I want to be clad in your own justice and receive from your love the possession of yourself."[12]

You cannot get into heaven by good works, but you also can't get in without good works, because faith without works is dead. Calvin put it in another riddle, "Salvation is by faith alone, but not by faith which is alone." Like Benedict, Thérèse trusts in grace, but that doesn't mean works are unnecessary or inconsequential. There is no room for complacency. She doesn't fall off either the Pelagian side of the horse or the Antinomian side. While the little way means total trust in God's grace, it also means we do our utmost to fulfill God's will. So she says:

> We must do everything that is within us: give without
> counting the cost, practice the virtues at every opportunity,

conquer ourselves all the time and prove our love by every
sort of tenderness and loving attention. In a word, we must
carry out all the good works that lie within our powers —
out of love for God. But it is truly essential to put our whole
trust in him who alone can sanctify our work, who can indeed sanctify us without works, since he may even bring
forth children of Abraham from the very stones. It is necessary for us, when we have done all we can to confess that we
are unprofitable servants, while hoping that God in his grace
will give us all that we need. That is the way of childhood.[13]

Her explanation of the grace-and-works conundrum is typi-
cally simple and profound: "Being little means not attributing
the virtues we practice to ourselves in the belief that we are ca-
pable of them, but recognising that the good God places this
treasure in the hands of his little child for him to use when necessary, but the treasure remains God's always."[14]

When Benedict calls his Rule a "little Rule for beginners,"
he states the secret of the whole Rule. The Benedictine way is a
"little way" because, like Thérèse of Lisieux's little way, it relies
on surrender, not superiority; grace, not greatness. For Benedict
and Thérèse heaven is not for heroes. Hans Urs Von Balthasar
points out that this little way is the only way "it differs from
other ways, above all from those of the 'great souls' who go in for
extraordinary penances and receive extraordinary mystical graces.
But, since neither the gospel nor the great saints themselves
reckon these latter as essential to Christian love, but recognize
that love of God and one's neighbour contains the whole of the
law, and all mysticism and asceticism, Thérèse's way which makes
this love absolutely central, can be described as *the* way."[15]

Not only does the little way of Benedict and Thérèse sum
up all the law and the prophets, not only does it carry in itself all

mysticism and asceticism, but it solves a whole library full of theological conundrums. The theologians who have pulled their beards and quarreled over the mysterious relationship between grace and works are answered in the simple teaching of Benedict and Thérèse. Those who have lain awake at night worrying over the nature of predestination and human free will can sleep easily with the little way in which God's children fulfill their own will by submitting to the Father's will. Grown-ups who debate the clashing demands of rules and freedom can relax. Benedict and Thérèse call for a kind of childhood in which perfect freedom is found in strict adherence to the rules.

If Father Benedict and Sister Thérèse silence the theologians, they silence the religious leaders too. All those who would divide the Church over grace or works, Scripture or Tradition, sacraments or word, service or sanctity, will be united in the wisdom of Benedict and Thérèse. If any Christian reads the two saints of the little way, they will also be united with every other disciple of Christ. Benedict draws all Christians together because he speaks from a time before the terrible divisions in Christ's Church. Thérèse unites Christians because her little doctrine of grace alone is a magnet to both Catholics and Protestants. Balthasar says, "One would have to be blind not to see that Thérèse's doctrine of the little way answers point by point the program outlined by the Reformers and that she presents the Church's bold, irrefutable answer to Protestant spirituality."[16]

Most importantly, Thérèse and Benedict draw Christians together because both saints point the believer to Christ himself. As G. K. Chesterton said in his biography of St. Francis, the saints may look like Christ, but Christ also looks like the saints. Likewise, the little way of Benedict and Thérèse is the way of Christ himself. As if he were following the little way, Christ surrendered totally to the Father's will. His teaching and his life were one, and Benedict and Thérèse simply echo their master. As Balthasar says, "Her way is the continuation of the gospel and the age-old tradition of the Church."[17]

When Benedict calls his teaching "a little Rule for beginners," there is more than one level of meaning. A beginner is an apprentice, a student who relies on his tutor. To learn he must listen, trust, and obey; but Benedict's "Rule for beginners" can take them all the way through life. Therefore his Rule is not just a place to begin but also a place to finish. To follow the way of Benedict and Thérèse is to be a beginner until the end. The one who really lives by faith can never do anything else, for "to walk by faith not by sight"[18] is to wander through life in a childlike state of wonder and willingness to learn. Henri Nouwen quotes a Zen master: "In the beginner's mind there is no thought, 'I have attained something.' All self-centred thought limits our vast soul. When we have no thought of achievement, no thought of self, we are true beginners. Then we can really learn something."[19]

Benedict's monastery is a "school for the Lord's service" and the emphasis is on "school." Therefore Benedict's Rule for beginners is a way for perpetual learners. In Benedict's family the old professed monk continues to be a fresh-eyed beginner just as much as the newest novice.

Thérèse knows she is a perpetual beginner. "I will be tormented by a foolish thing I said or did, then I turn to myself and say, Ah, still standing at the same spot as at the beginning!"[20] Balthasar explains this phenomenon another way:

> Perhaps this is the shortest formula we have for the little way. It is both endlessly humiliating and endlessly encouraging; humiliating because one is forever going through the same movements without ever reaching the

goal — encouraging because even one's tentative move-
ments have not separated one from the source, one's growth
has not been false and one remains in communication with
the eternal springs.[21]

Part of the littleness of Benedict's Rule is how mundane it
all is. The Rule is one of the classics of European literature, and
yet on its first reading it seems quite unremarkable. Indeed, much
of the Rule seems overly concerned with religious routine and
the petty details of daily life. Twelve out of seventy-three chapters are devoted to detailed instructions on how and when to
perform the Daily Office. Thus the ordinary reader is regaled
with such dull passages as:

> On ordinary days the solemn Office of Lauds is to be
> carried out as follows: Psalm 66 is to be said without an
> antiphon, and rather slowly (as on Sunday) so that all may
> arrive in time for Psalm 50 which is to be chanted with an
> antiphon. After this let two more Psalms be chanted, keep-
> ing to custom: meaning, on Monday 5 and 35, on Tuesday
> 42 and 56.[22]

And so on for many chapters more. Fourteen chapters deal
with the fiddly details of monastic discipline: who should be
punished, how they should be treated, and when they may be
restored. Another sixteen chapters deal with minutiae like: how
the monks should sleep, how much food and drink they should
have, when they should eat, what their footwear and clothing
should be like, and how they should use the tools of the monastery. The Rule deals with how kitchen duty should be done, how
boys should be disciplined, and who should look after those in
the infirmary. This hardly sounds like one of the most exalted

spiritual texts of all time; but it is in this attention to ordinary detail that Benedict is showing the heart of his little Rule. By focusing on the mundane matters of everyday life Benedict points to a deeper truth: that these details are the stuff of reality, and that by paying attention to the details of ordinary life we will find our way to heaven. Someone has said the devil is in the details; Benedict thinks the divine is in the details.

If the first-time reader has to struggle with the mundane minutiae of sixth-century monastic life in Benedict, then in Thérèse he has to struggle with an even more difficult dose of "ordinariness." At least there is some historical interest in reading about the sleeping arrangements of sixth-century monks, but Thérèse takes us into the detailed life of the nineteenth-century French bourgeoisie. Her writings are full of spiritual points made through the events of ordinary days. So we are plunged into the details of visits to relatives, a first train ride, trips to the seaside, and the traumas of a little girl's school days. We are told about playtime with her sisters, quarrels with the maid, and the joy of cuddles with Mommy and Daddy. Those who are looking for a lofty spiritual treatise will find in both Benedict and Thérèse a hefty dose of ordinary life instead.

There is another aspect to Benedict and Thérèse's littleness that irks the sophisticated reader. The stories of Benedict and Thérèse are not ashamed of the more embarrassing aspects of popular religion. All that makes sophisticates cringe about religion is there in its gaudy glory in Benedict and Thérèse. So Gregory the Great's biography of Benedict revels in the larger-than-life legends of miracles and extreme asceticism that surrounded the holy man. The up-to-date reader may pooh-pooh the miracles of Benedict, but they are part of his ordinary appeal. The story of St. Benedict makes the point that the most miraculous thing about miracles is that they are ordinary. That is to say they are an ordinary part of religion, and any religion without miracles is not ordinary religion. In fact, religion without miracles is probably not religion at all but some form of positive thinking, and what is positive thinking except a form of wishful thinking?

Why do people dismiss miracles? Perhaps they sincerely believe such things do not happen; but, in our day, alleged miracles are all too frequent. We are surrounded by miracle-working evangelists, Charismatic Christians whose teeth fill up with gold when they pray, Buddhists who levitate, Hindu statues that drink milk, apparitions of the Blessed Virgin, and messages to housewives from aliens and angels. If people dismiss miracles, perhaps it is because they are bored with them. Even scientists today accept that weird and wonderful things do happen, and that in itself is a kind of miracle. What people cannot and will not do is draw conclusions from miracles. They know odd events do not prove anything. Miracles may bolster faith, but they do not force belief.

Nevertheless, the intellectually pious are still inclined to dismiss miracles. Using the professional sleight of hand of "reinterpretation" they hope the miracles will miraculously disappear. This academic denial is not only dull but debatable; and very often the "reinterpretation" of the miracle is more incredible than the miracle itself. Why can't the open-minded be open-minded about miracles? To be embarrassed by them and say they didn't happen is such a predictable and timid response. What is most disturbing is that those who seem to doubt miracles the most are often the religious professionals. No wonder no one wants to go to church anymore if the churchmen are so dull.

To speak plainly, the main problem for sophisticated people is not that miracles are incredible, but that they are an error in taste. To profess belief in miracles takes one perilously close to faith healers, the souvenir stalls of Lourdes, and lurid pictures of Jesus with googly eyes. There is a breed of spiritually minded people who reduce Christianity to the highest form of aesthetics. Beauty leads us to Truth, but beauty without truth is false, and that which is false and beautiful does not remain beautiful for very long. If the faith is no more than a pretty face, then the aesthetes are also atheists. Since miracles are an error in taste, it is far more subversive and therefore far more Christian to accept the miracles. It's also much more fun — rather like wearing a hideous hat on purpose.

If Benedict's biography gives the sophisticated soul miracles to stumble over, then Thérèse's story gives tasteful grown-ups an even bigger obstacle. To find Thérèse, the modern soul has to climb over the stumbling block of her style. We modern-day pilgrims are presented with a nineteenth-century teenage nun with a pretty smile and schoolgirl enthusiasms. She speaks in language that seems archaic and sickly sweet. Among other sentimental touches she calls herself a little flower of Jesus and a little ball for the child Jesus to play with. She thinks God is her "Papa" and likens herself to a bowl of milk that kittens come to drink from. It's easy to turn away such greeting-card spirituality in distaste, but this is precisely the first test. Thérèse swamps tasteful people with sentimentality and sweetness, and only when they survive the taste test can they begin to appreciate her wisdom. She is one of the best examples of the secret Catholic truth that says the tasteful cannot enter the kingdom of heaven.

We are told that in great art, form should be appropriate to content. In Thérèse the two meet very happily. Her theme is the little way of spiritual childhood, so it is appropriate that she writes in a childlike style. Her gushing scribblings are almost like those of any other adolescent girl who keeps a diary, and should be read as such. Those who do not appreciate her style will probably not be able to appreciate her content either. But what we most dislike may be the very thing that would do us the most good. What the grumpiest old grown-up needs is a dose of childhood.

Her critics say Thérèse encourages others to live in a never-never land of spiritual unreality — a rose garden where everything is cozy and sweet. Those who have read her work and studied her life realize that beneath the sweetness there is light. Thérèse never avoids the grim realities, and if she offers roses, those roses have real thorns. Thérèse's sentimentality is more of a fluke than a fault. She simply speaks in the language of her time and place. While her style is sometimes sentimental, "Thérèse ruthlessly kicks aside all the heaps of pious, well-meant untruths,"[23] saying, "In Carmel one is not allowed to strike false coins to buy souls."[24] Thérèse suffers gladly, but she does not suffer fools gladly. When a sister prophesied that a company of radiant white angels would be present at her deathbed, Thérèse replies, "All these images mean nothing to me. I can only nourish myself on the Truth."[25] Thérèse's insistence on Truth is reminiscent of a child's remorseless questioning as well as every child's innate dislike for hypocrisy and humbug.

Benedict and Thérèse call us to follow a little way, and it may be that for humility to begin growing, our grown-up taste must be the first to go. Miracles, relics, sentimentality, pilgrimages, and wonderful answers to prayer lie at the heart of ordinary religion, and since Benedict and Thérèse are apostles of the ordinary it is fitting that their religion sits happily among the sentimental, the miraculous, and the tasteless. It is part of their way to be little, and to be little means to accept the ridiculous particularities of religion with the abandon of a child with a party bag full of cheap trinkets and sweets. Thérèse says to her sister, "You are very little, and when one is little one does not have beautiful thoughts."[26] This does not mean we should despise the great glories of liturgy, music, art, and architecture, which the Catholic religion offers. It simply means that if a religion is universal it will find room for both the sentimental and the sublime.

Benedict and Thérèse call ordinary Christians to extraordinary perfection — not by being extraordinarily perfect, but by being perfectly ordinary. Being ordinary means letting go every vestige of snobbery and learning that we are not special after all. Once we grasp this troublesome truth it is easy to make the mistake of thinking that "being ordinary" means fitting in and becoming "one of the boys." While being ordinary has nothing to do with snobbery it also has nothing to do with being one of the crowd. Snobbery has destroyed many lives through its snooty pride, but the reverse snobbery that will do anything to "fit in" and be part of the *hoi polloi* is also destructive. It is just as artificial for the aristocrat to affect working-class manners as it is for the social climber to put on an upper-class accent. In that sense, being common is just as false as being uncommon. Being ordinary means being none other than who we are. As a result it is just as possible for a duchess to be as ordinary as a dustman.

The most insidious way of trying to be extraordinary is by being extraordinarily religious. Religion that seeks an escape from the ordinary world is false religion, but if the "ordinary" world is false, then running away from it may be the truest thing to do. Thomas Merton observes how those most extraordinary men — the Desert Fathers — actually went out to the desert to be ordinary:

> These monks insisted on remaining human and ordinary. This may seem to be a paradox, but it is very important. If we reflect a moment, we will see that to fly into the desert in order to be extraordinary is only to carry the world

with you as an implicit standard of comparison. The result would be nothing but self-contemplation, and self-comparison with the negative standard of the world one had abandoned. . . . The simple men who lived their lives out to a good old age among the rocks and sands only did so because they had come into the desert to be themselves, their ordinary selves, and to forget a world that divided them from themselves. There can be no other valid reason for seeking solitude or for leaving the world.[27]

It is difficult to see how someone like St. Simeon the Stylite was ordinary. In the fifth century he went out to the Syrian desert and chose to live on top of a sixty-foot-high pillar. He liked it so much he stayed there for the next thirty-five years. St. Simeon seems bizarre, but what is bizarre for one person is ordinary to another. I find it bizarre that grown men are paid exorbitant amounts of money to run around a field in short trousers trying to kick a ball into a net, but millions of people think soccer is quite a sane and ordinary pastime. Chesterton said, "There is more simplicity in a man who eats caviar because he likes it than in a man who eats grape-nuts out of conviction." St. Simeon was ordinary because for him praying on top of a pillar for thirty-five years was the most natural thing in the world. Likewise, Benedict and Thérèse follow their religious lives because they want to, not because they ought to. The religious life is their way of being ordinary, and it delights them. Benedict follows the way with "a sweetness beyond words"[28] and Thérèse realizes in all simplicity that what she desires is what God wants for her: "God made me always desire what he wanted to give me."[29]

Monks and nuns are commonly thought of as spiritual elitists, but one of Benedict's great contributions to the monastic tradition was to draw it back from extremes. He will not lay down anything that is "harsh or hard to bear."[30] His monks were cut off from the world in some ways, but their communities were also integrated into the wider world. Their basic lifestyle was simply that of the other subsistence farmers with whom they lived. Benedict was never a priest, and he envisioned his monasteries as communities of laymen. Benedict's Rule is not an esoteric treatise that ushers the devotee into mystic realms through the mastery of arcane knowledge and bizarre asceticism. Benedict is no yogi. His Rule is a practical guide for ordinary men and women to follow Christ perfectly by living together in community. As such, its principles can be applied to laypeople, families, and every Christian community.

While it is enclosed, the Carmelite convent is also not elitist or extraordinary. The contemplative life is a vital and ordinary part of the whole Church. If the Church is a body, then the enclosed contemplative orders can be likened to the heart, beating with the liturgy and alive with a passion that vitalizes the whole body of Christ. Thérèse saw her entry into the convent as the most natural thing to do. She also thought her "little way" was for ordinary people. She says the publication of her biography "will be useful to all kinds of souls, apart from those who take extraordinary measures."[31]

Benedict and Thérèse call us to find ourselves in ordinary life. The little way for beginners lies open before everyone, for the path leads through the real demands and details of everyday community life. The family, the school, the parish, and the workplace can all be "schools of the Lord's service."[32] Because Thérèse and Benedict know God is present in the ordinary life, their vision transforms mundane existence. Suddenly every moment shines with the possibility of heaven and surges with potential joy. This understanding infuses Benedict and Thérèse with a rush of energy, so with great vigor Benedict calls on his brothers and sisters, "Let us rouse ourselves . . . run while you have the light of life. . . . If we wish to make our home in the dwelling place of his Kingdom, there will be no getting there unless we run towards it by good deeds."[33] Thérèse also radiates a magnificent vitality. She calls each Christian with youthful enthusiasm, saying, "In order to be holy, the most essential virtue is energy. With energy one can easily reach the height of perfection."[34] "You cannot be half a saint," she cries. "You must be a whole saint or no saint at all!"[35]

Chapter Two Endnotes

1. Abbot Parry (tr.), *The Rule of St. Benedict*, Leominster, Gracewing, 1997, p. 118.
2. Ibid.
3. Ibid., p. 2.
4. Ibid., p. 4.
5. Ibid.
6. Ephesians 2:8-9.
7. Parry, p. 1.
8. Ibid., p. 40.
9. Ibid., p. 3.
10. Ibid.
11. Ibid., p. 4.
12. John Clarke O.C.D. (tr.), *The Story of a Soul: The Autobiography of St. Thérèse of Lisieux*, Washington, D.C., ICS Publications, 1976, p. 277.
13. I. F. Görres, *The Hidden Face: A Study of St. Thérèse of Lisieux*, New York, Pantheon, 1959, pp. 281-282.
14. Thomas N. Taylor (tr.), *Saint Thérèse of Lisieux, The Little Flower of Jesus*, New York, P. J. Kenedy, 1926, pp. 295-296.
15. Hans Urs Von Balthasar, *Two Sisters in the Spirit*, San Francisco, Ignatius Press, 1970, p. 298.
16. Ibid., p. 283.
17. Ibid.
18. 2 Corinthians 5:7.

19. Shunryu Suzuki, *Zen Mind, Beginner's Mind,* T. Dixon (ed.), New York, Weatherill, 1970, p. 18. Quoted in Nouwen, *Genesee Diary,* p. 172.

20. John Clarke O.C.D. (tr.), *St. Thérèse of Lisieux: Her Last Conversations,* Washington, D.C., ICS Publications, 1977, pp. 73-74.

21. Balthasar, p. 148.

22. Parry, p. 35.

23. Balthasar, p. 46.

24. Clarke, *[St. Thérèse's] Last Conversations,* p. 82.

25. Ibid., p. 134.

26. Ibid., p. 218.

27. Thomas Merton, *The Wisdom of the Desert,* London, Sheldon Press, 1960, p. 22.

28. Parry, p. 4.

29. Clarke, *[St. Thérèse's] Last Conversations,* p. 94.

30. Parry, p. 4.

31. H. Petitot, O.P., *Saint Thérèse de Lisieux: Une Renaissance spirituelle,* Paris, Desclée, 1925, p. 91.

32. Parry, p. 4.

33. Ibid., p. 2.

34. John Clarke, O.C.D. (tr.), *General Correspondence, Vol. II,* Washington, D.C., ICS Publications, 1988, p. 909.

35. Ibid., p. 1133.

Three

The Way
of the Lamb

Thoughts and Prayers

Whoever is little let him come to me.

— PROVERBS 9:4

Truly, I say to you, unless you turn and become like children, you will never enter the kingdom of heaven.

— MATTHEW 18:3

The mysteries of the kingdom are fittingly revealed to mere babes because babes, unlike grown-ups who think they know every-thing, are ready to receive the truth.

— JOHN SAWARD

Around the child bend all the three
Sweet Graces, Faith, Hope and Charity.

— WALTER LANDOR

even if it's sunday may I be wrong,
for whenever men are right they are not young.

— E. E. CUMMINGS

Prayer
Lord of Creation! I do not know how to pray. I do not know what to say. I give you the entire prayer book.

— AN ANONYMOUS JEWISH BOY

Villiam Blake asked, "Little lamb, who made thee? . . . / Little lamb, I'll tell thee, / He is called by thy name, / For he calls himself a Lamb. / He is meek, and he is mild; / He became a little child." Authentic poets are also prophets; as Elijah sat under a tree and was fed by angels, Blake sat in a tree and saw angels. Like the second Elijah (John the Baptist), Blake points his finger toward the Lamb of God. One who points his finger is pointing the way, so when Blake points us to the Lamb he also tells us to follow the Lamb. Jesus tells the story of the Good Shepherd, but as the priest is also the victim, so the Shepherd of God is also the Lamb of God. As a result, those who follow the Good Shepherd also follow the Lamb. Indeed, the book of Revelation proclaims this paradox when it says the martyrs are those "who follow the Lamb wherever he goes; . . . the Lamb in the midst of the throne will be their shepherd."[1]

The Lamb "became a little child," and if we want to follow him we must become as little children. Benedict called his Rule a "little Rule," and a little rule is for little people. Children are little people, and it is no coincidence that Benedict calls his monks "sons." The opening words of his Rule are, "Listen, my son . . . turn the ear of your heart to the advice of a loving father."[2] If his disciples are sons, then they are children. Many observers have commented on the extraordinary youthfulness of monks and nuns, but their childlike quality is never an embarrassing immaturity. An aging monk who is youthful is not at all like an aging executive who combs his hair over, wears jeans, and drives a sports car. Benedict's children are not a band of lost boys who never grow up; rather, they are adopted sons who have found a Father. The Peter Pans of this world are perpetually immature; Benedict's sons are perpetually innocent. Peter Pan's wish never to grow up is a fairy tale of twisted desire with a hook in the end. Benedict's sons follow another Peter — one who was so childlike that he stepped out of his boat to walk on the raging sea to meet the Captain of his soul.

Because Benedict writes as a father to his children, his "little Rule" can be seen as a way of spiritual childhood. The "little way," which is implicit in Benedict's Rule, shines clearly in Thérèse. She writes, "The Little Way is the way of spiritual childhood, the way of trust and total surrender. To remain little means recognizing one's nothingness."[3] Elsewhere she wrote, "He wishes me to surrender myself like a little child and not concern myself over what is to happen to me."[4]

John Saward explains Thérèse's "little way of spiritual childhood":

> First, let us make clear what it is not. It is not childishness, the refusal to grow up, that psychological heresy which Chesterton dubbed 'Peter Pantheism.' In the early hours of Christmas Day 1886 Thérèse was given what she called the 'grace of my complete conversion' which was at the same time, the 'grace of leaving my childhood.' One might say she gave up one childhood for another: she left behind natural childhood, which is but a passing state, in order to make more intensely her own the supernatural childhood of her Baptism. . . . Here is the paradox of the Gospel. It is only when we convert and become like little children that we reach our Christian maturity.[5]

"Ah," we say, "the little way of the Lamb is indeed a beautiful idea, and doubtless it is the way some are called to." But with the Gospel, Thérèse insists that this is not a way, but *the* way. To follow the Lamb and become a child is not an option; it is a command. "Unless you turn and become like children," says the Gospel, "you will never enter the kingdom of heaven."[6]

"No grown-ups allowed" reads the sign over the door into paradise. Pearls are tiny, and so are the pearly gates. When Jesus
said the way was narrow, perhaps he meant it was too narrow
for grown-ups to squeeze through. The grown-ups are camels
— hairy, lumpy, over-burdened, bad-tempered brutes — who
can never get through that eye of a needle that is the little door
of heaven.

To become like a child is to share in the mystery of
Bethlehem, where the Creator himself became a child. As Saward
puts it, "The Son came from the Father by the Little Way, as a
child, and by the Little Way, as children, we are led by Him to
the Father."[7] It is no mistake that Thérèse is called Sister Thérèse
of the Child Jesus, for her life and teaching are a vivid reminder
that in becoming a child, Christ fulfilled his own precept that
"unless you become a child you cannot enter the kingdom."
Saward sums it up, "By becoming the child of the Virgin, the
eternal son of the Father raises all natural childhood to a new
and wonderful dignity and opens up for us the way of spiritual
childhood, as adopted children of God."[8]

Father Benedict also encourages us to become spiritual children, for at the heart of his little Rule is the monk's childlike
relationship with his abbot. Through his earthly father in God
the monk is mysteriously linked to his heavenly Father, God.
Benedict affirms this sacrament in his instructions to the abbot,
who in his very name is an abba-father. "An abbot . . . must always bear in mind what he is called . . . for he is believed to act
in the place of Christ in the monastery since he is called by his
title, as the Apostle says, 'You have received the Spirit of adop-
tion as sons, through whom we cry Abba Father!' "[9]

To become a spiritual child presupposes the existence of the
spiritual father. Benedict cannot be an abba-father if his monks
will not be sons, and Thérèse cannot be a daughter if she does

not have a father. So Thérèse says, the little way means "expecting everything of the Good God, just as a little child expects
everything of his father."[10] It means believing the words of St.
Paul, that "all things work together for good for those who trust
God." Thérèse writes, "Since we wish to be little children . . .
little children do not know what is best; they find everything
good. Let us copy them."[11] Does this sound ridiculous? With a
sly subversiveness Thérèse adds, "Besides, there is no merit in
doing what is reasonable."[12]

How we view the world depends on our parents because in
infancy our parents are our world. They are the life source, the
ground of our being, and our introduction to the wider world.
Mother and father play a complementary role in childhood.
Through the mother the child is linked with his physical and
emotional needs. We are attached to our mother, and through
her we learn how to be attached to all things. The father, on the
other hand, is the focus of our psychological and spiritual needs.
He is detached, and from him we learn to be detached from all
things. In a natural home the mother is subjective, intimate, and
physical; the father is objective, detached, and spiritual. Together
they nurture a well-rounded child — an individual who is both
physical and spiritual, intellectual and emotional, loving and yet
detached. St. Paul tells us the relationship between man and
wife reflects that between Christ and his Church. Likewise, Jesus
teaches that the relationship between father and child reflects
the love between God the Father and God the Son. That relationship, within the intimacy of the Most Holy Trinity, draws
all the adopted children of Adam into the Father's embrace.

Benedict saw a mysterious link between the abbot and the
heavenly Father. Thérèse and her natural sisters were blessed
with a tender and spiritual father. No wonder Thérèse looked to
M. Martin as an image of her heavenly Father. Soon after her

arrival at the convent she writes, "When I think of you, my dearest little Father, I naturally think of the good God, for it seems to me to be impossible to see anyone on earth holier than you."[13] Just as her Lord called the heavenly Father *abba*, or Papa, so Thérèse thinks of God as her heavenly Papa. On her deathbed she said, "Don't worry if you find me dead one morning. It'll just be because Papa the Good God has come to look for me."[14] When her father died, Thérèse was bold enough to write, "The good God has taken away the one whom we have loved so tenderly. Did this not happen so that we might say in all truth, 'Our Father, who art in heaven'?"[15]

The relationship between the father and child is mysterious and fascinating. At first the child is one with its mother. Father is the distant big voice — the significant other. He is an image of all that exists beyond the warm enclosure of the mother's embrace. As such he must be a focus of fear, because we are all afraid of the unknown. Before long, the feared father is the lawgiver. In a patriarchal home, whether he really does or not, father knows best. Here is a terrible twist: the child needs to rebel against this false father to find freedom. Oh, fortunate sin! The rebellion is a kind of horrible necessity, for how can the child return to the father unless he first goes away? How can he really love the father unless he first rejects him? The most terrible thing about this rejection of the father is the very real risk that the child may never return. Still the call of the father echoes in the human heart. No matter what swine we live with, the father remains the still point in the turning world — the one from whom we run and the one to whom we must all one day return — either in rebellion or in reconciliation.

This individual mystery is reflected in the universal story of the Hebrew people. At first God is the Creator, the Great Other. Then he is the lawgiver and the voice from the mountain. From the pillar of fire he leads his children through the desert to the promised land. From there they drift into rebellion, and through the prophets he calls, "Oh, my people, what have I done to you?" Jesus Christ summed up the whole drama in his story of the prodigal son. There in the mystery of rebellion and return the child becomes a man, then, in returning, becomes a child again; but his new childhood holds a new maturity. Because it is experienced, innocence restored is more innocent than innocence never lost. The Gospel command to become as little children is a call to return to the state of innocence through the excruciating path of experience. In the drama of rebellion and return, the sons of Adam relearn the wisdom their father forgot. They end up wiser than Adam because in the second Adam they have what their father had, but have conquered hell to find it.

From Abraham and Isaac to Prospero and Miranda, from Daedalus and Icarus to Rigoletto and Gilda, the heartrending relationship between father and child burns in the heart of every man. The little way of the Lamb is the way of the father and child together. Christ can only expect us to become spiritual children because the Father is there for us. If the Lord is not also the Father, then Christ is calling us to be orphans and foundlings. To be a spiritual child presupposes the heavenly Father's love, and if we cannot relate to God as a child to a father, it will be difficult to relate to him at all.

That the relationship between father and child is a dynamic image of the spiritual way makes some grown-ups howl, for they have grown to hate both children and fathers. The extreme feminists have fabricated the fantastic falsehood that all fathers are abusers of women and children and that patriarchy is inherently evil. Everyone agrees that bad fathers are bad, but even if every father is bad, it doesn't destroy the idea that good fathers are a good thing. Anti-patriarchal propaganda has wormed its way into Christian feminism as well. The father-phobes have succeeded in turning Thérèse's "good God" into a bad God, and God the Father has become God the monster. The God of our fathers who is himself our Father has been made an outcast. The patriarch is a pariah. He is a divorced Dad — cast out of the family home and onto the streets.

Unfortunately for those who hate fathers, patriarchy is part of the Judeo-Christian story. It is therefore part of the divine revelation. As such it is integral to the whole plan, and those feminists who abandon Christianity as "inherently patriarchal" are honest to do so. But while they return to the Earth Mother, Christians, like the prodigal, will return to the father and the family because they remain a profound and necessary image of God the Father and the Holy Trinity itself.

The grown-up theologian dismisses the idea of God the Father with a smile, saying, "Ah, but we now know that God, whatever that concept may mean, transcends our finite conceptualizations of sexuality. To call God 'Father' is mere anthropomorphism." To call God "Father" is indeed anthropomorphism, but is anthropomorphism necessarily a bad thing? Which is a better way to think of the unthinkable — that he is a heavenly Father or that he is "the life essence of the cosmos"? With the first I may imagine a loving Being greater than myself with whom I may enter a relationship. With the second, as C. S. Lewis has pointed out, I can only imagine a vast tapioca pudding in the sky.[16]

God may be the heavenly Father, but we all know that while he is not less than that, he is certainly far more than that. Calling God "Father" not only opens up his identity as Father, but it opens the way to a far more expansive view of God as well. Because a metaphor is poetry, it both limits and expands language at the same time. Thérèse is a good example of an ordinary person's open-minded use of metaphor. Her language is quaint, but her thought is both wide and deep. She endorses patriarchy with delight, but she also knows that God's Fatherhood is far greater than mere human sexuality. Julian of Norwich is famous for realizing that "verily as God is our Father he is also our Mother," and her sister Thérèse embraces the same truth. When considering God's quickness to forgive, she writes, "God is more tender than a mother."[17] Always one to stand things on their head, Thérèse learned how a father can be a mother from her own earthly father. Of M. Martin she says, "Papa's compassionate nature made him a mother as well as a father to me."[18] But Thérèse and Julian would not have claimed a new discovery in this strange motherly kind of fatherhood. That most patriarchal of documents, the Old Testament, knows that God is also like a mother. Thérèse loves to quote God's words through the prophet Isaiah: "As one whom a mother caresses, so will I comfort you; you shall be carried at the breasts and upon the knees they shall caress you."[19]

Psychologists tell us one of the father's natural roles is to help his children develop their sexual identity. Because the father is the first man the girl will ever know, he helps develop her feminine reactions to the masculine. The son — who is first joined to a woman, his mother — learns to separate and become a man through his relationship with his father. If there is no father or the fathering is faulty, sexual confusion is the result. Thérèse and Benedict offer the little way of childhood, a way that calls us to live in relationship with the heavenly Father. In a world of sexual confusion and fear, this little way can be a path of healing and wholeness.

The father-child relationship, which is integral to the "little way," is always set in a context of a whole family. As a result the family becomes the focus of salvation. Only within a whole family can the whole person develop naturally and innocently. In a faithful marriage, man and woman live a mythical reality — restoring in daily life what Adam and Eve soiled by selfishness in Eden. Within the family, fathers may live with daughters, and mothers with sons, in a chaste and mysterious relationship of trust and mutual self-giving. Tertullian called marriage the "seminary of the human race." He might just as well have said that the family is the monastery of the human race, for there we make lifelong vows to live together in chastity, obedience, and poverty of spirit.

Thérèse regarded the domestic family as an icon of the heavenly community itself, and Benedict certainly sees his monastery as a little Christian family. Within the web of community life, with all its stresses and demands, Benedict and Thérèse find the relationships that connect them to God. They would say the same can be found in an ordinary Christian family. Balthasar sums it up:

> Without in any way turning the family into a monastery, the truly Christian family will allow the light of God to permeate every natural event and attachment so that they all become symbolic of Christ and the Church; thus the effect of the sacraments, their transforming power is felt in the smallest, everyday incidents. The Christian family must be a reflection of the Holy Family which is itself the type of the supernatural Christian family.[20]

The family becomes a glimpse of eternal communion, and learning to live together here below is a preparation for living together there above.

The security of the family provides freedom for the child. Because he is secure he is free to engage in that most unself-

conscious and childlike activity: play. The little child plays naturally and naturally plays. As John Saward points out, "According
to St. Thomas Aquinas, following Aristotle, playfulness is a natural virtue, and too little play a vice."[21] When a child of any age
plays naturally, he is being fully human. If the simple glory of
humanity shines at playtime, so does the simple glory of God,
for Thomas Aquinas and the writer of the Negro spiritual both
thought God was playing when he held the whole world in his
hands. Certainly the image of God forming man from the clay
of the earth sounds like an eight-year-old making little mud
men. Since play is human and divine, those charming images of
the child Jesus playing ball with John the Baptist may be the
ones that best illustrate the union of his divine and human natures.

Thérèse refers to herself as the "ball of the child Jesus."[22]
She wrote plays and acted in them. Indeed, for her, praying is
playing. She sees her vocation as playing in the court of Christ
the King like some princess in a fairy tale:

> I, as the baby of the family, will stay close to the King's
> throne . . . and go on loving on behalf of my brothers out
> on the battle field. This love of mine, how to show it? Well,
> even a little child can scatter flowers to scent the throne
> room with their fragrance, even a little child can sing, in
> its shrill treble, the great canticle of love . . . and so the
> church in heaven, ready to take part in the childish game I
> am playing will begin scattering these flowers on the souls
> in Purgatory . . . scatter them on the church militant and
> give her the strength for fresh conquests.[23]

Not to play is to be grown-up. All work and no play does
not make Jack a dull boy — it makes him no boy at all. It is

grown-ups who are workaholics. As Balthasar points out, "While the grown up groans beneath the curse of the toil that comes from original sin, the child busies himself with play, which originates in Paradise and is a creaturely reflection of God's creative busy-ness."[24]

The way of spiritual childhood leaves the busy-ness of business to others. Instead of making money, the spiritual person — no matter what his job — is intent on making things and people. Inasmuch as he is being creative, he is playing. This kind of work matches the Benedictine ideal. If Thérèse thinks play and prayer are one, Benedict thinks work and prayer are one. If work can be prayer and play can be prayer, it follows that work can be play.

This is a conundrum that simply means that when the monk works he is both praying and playing. Thomas Merton glimpsed this ideal in one of his first visits to the Trappist monastery. He writes:

> For the good Trappist work is important. It is a mixture of penance and recreation. However hard it is, it is still a form of play. Even the strictest penance is play too. The liturgy, too. The Trappist uses work to save his soul. To be as little as children, we must play like them, do things not because they are physically necessary, but freely, as if almost arbitrarily for love. Behind the strictness of Trappist discipline is this complete metaphysical freedom from physical necessity that makes it a kind of play.[25]

The child at play is not self-conscious, but he is self-confident. He leaps and runs with carefree abandon and boundless energy. Thérèse says, "In order to be holy the most essential virtue is energy."[26] With the psalmist she wants to run in the way of God's commandments, and with Benedict she says to the Lord, "I run with delight in the way of Your new Commandment."[27] Benedict sees the spiritual life with the same vitality. All through the Rule he encourages his monks to "run in the path." Running is both exhausting and exhilarating. If Benedict calls his disciples to be like athletes, he never wants them to forget the joy of the long-distance runner. Athletes run to win. Children run for fun. Like children whooping with joy as they chase each other down a hill, the monks are to run on the path "filled with the inexpressible delight of love." They are like lambs leaping and dashing about the hillside or, as the psalmist sings, they are like young deer skipping in high places.

The Gospel is never good news unless it is subversive, and what could be more subversive to a world of grown-ups than the call to become as playful little children? Shall we become like little lambs skipping and gamboling on the hillside in spring? Surely this is the worst kind of mawkish mock-mysticism. One shrinks from the sentimentality and bad taste of it all. In a world of sophisticated somebodies, what a scandal to be a nobody! In a world of grown-ups, how ridiculous to be a child! But then the tables are turned by the one who first turned over the tables in the temple. There is a cruel irony and a harsh paradox in the thought of becoming a lamb: from the mysterious stories of Abraham and Moses onward, both the son and the innocent lamb are the ideal sacrifice. At the climax of human history the two terrible images unite as the Son of God is led out like a lamb to the slaughter. To be a lamb is to be a victim. To follow the Lamb means taking up a cross. It is no mistake that Thérèse constantly reminded her sisters that her title was not only Thérèse of the Child Jesus but also of the Holy Face. Her devotion to the face of the crucified Lord and to the child Jesus illustrates how the way of the Lamb is the way of sacrifice.

To become a child in our grown-up world is like sauntering into a pack of wolves wearing lambskin, for there is nothing in our society more twisted and threatening than our approach to childhood. We are churlish about chastity and insulting toward innocence. Like all decadent societies we have sentimentalized and destroyed childhood at the same time. We deplore pedophilia, yet we dish out "value-free" sex education and consider teen sex a healthy form of recreation. When it comes to producing new children, we hail the latest chemicals and gadgets to produce conception while dishing out more chemicals and gadgets to prevent conception. We campaign to save baby seals and tortoises while we "eliminate" street children in the slums and "terminate" our unborn sons and daughters. We want to preserve creation in national parks while we're busy perverting creation in the genetic laboratories. To sum it up, we are pro-creation in every area but procreation.

"What a brave new world that has such creatures in it!" cries the innocent child Miranda. If only there were something brave or new about it. For children, the twenty-first century is as cowardly and old as Herod. John Saward quotes Balthasar that "everywhere outside Christianity the child is automatically sacrificed,"[28] and likens our slaughter of the innocents to the children sacrificed to the Canaanite monster Moloch. We recoil at the idea of gibbering devotees of a bloodthirsty god; but through history the killing of children was not only the preserve of savages. The sophisticated have always disdained childhood. Plato regarded children as half-finished human beings, and Aristotle, like the United Nations and the Nazis, advocated population control by abortion. In ancient Rome, infanticide and abortion were commonplace. The second-century *Didache* says Christians stood out because they "do not corrupt boys and murder children by abortion or after birth." In every sub-Christian culture the child is a subhuman object for experimentation and extermination. Whether the killing is clean and clinical or bloody and barbaric is only a matter of form. British mystic Patricia de Menezes sees the millions of aborted unborn as Holy Innocents or "crucified innocents." They are the ones who, like Christ, are led out like lambs to the slaughter.[29] She is courageous enough to suggest that by some mystery written in the deep magic before time, the slaughtered unborn are valuable victims in the divine economy. God may wrest from our selfish slaughter more souls to stand before the throne of the Lamb. If this is so, then instead of being disposable they become indispensable. Like a horrific Grünewald crucifix, the annihilated unborn suddenly become the gruesome icons of our redemption and our destiny. If one is to follow Benedict and Thérèse in the way of spiritual childhood, then it means becoming, like them, innocent victims. The mind is drawn to the unforgettable image of a terrified Jewish boy from the Warsaw ghetto, hands raised at the end of a Nazi rifle. There is the child of our age. He is the sacrificial lamb. To follow the Lamb is not only to sympathize with that boy but also to become one with him. As in the Book of Revelation, "following the Lamb" means pursuing our ultimate destiny to the altar of the cross.

Thérèse's writing about sacrifice takes her to the brink of a vast mystery. Early in her life she says, "I felt a great desire for suffering spring up in my heart, together with the conviction that our Lord had a lot of crosses in store for me. I was carried away on a tide of happiness which I shall always look on as one of the greatest graces I ever received."[30]

Elsewhere she writes, "Yes, suffering stretched out its arms toward me, and I threw myself into them with love."[31] A month before her death she said, "No, I am not an angel. The angels cannot suffer, they are not so fortunate as I."[32] What might be a weird pathological condition in a lesser soul is a clear and dazzling revelation of truth from Thérèse. To be human is not only to err but also to suffer. The child Thérèse believes that in her sacrificial suffering she has become fully human. Thérèse is not insane. She has simply realized that suffering takes one to the heart of the human condition, and there at the cross, reality — and therefore God — is found. Balthasar says she raised the point of suffering sacrifice to the highest level of human existence: "In her view, suffering is the summit of a creature's attainments, the most precious gift of God and the most precious offering that a creature can give back to him. Suffering, for a person who loves God, is the height of existence."[33] Descartes said, "I think, therefore I am." Thérèse answers, "I suffer, therefore I am."

In the end Thérèse made a heroic sacrifice. Her painful death, combined with a terrible spiritual darkness, took her into a full identification with the Lamb of God; but in keeping with her little way, she never aspired to a sensational sacrifice. The way of the Lamb was found through the daily routine of self-sacrificial living. "Sensational acts of piety are not for me — this shall be my life, to miss no single opportunity of making some small sacrifice, here by a smiling look, there by a kindly word, always doing the tiniest things right and doing it for love."[34]

Benedict is no less intent on the life of sacrifice. Like Thérèse, he eschews sensational acts of piety. Instead his little Rule for beginners places sacrifice at the heart of daily life. St. Paul spoke of "dying daily" and told the faithful to offer their bodies as a "living sacrifice."[35] Through routine obedience the monk does exactly that. Benedict writes in chapter five:

> Thus they take the narrow way, as the Lord says, 'Narrow is the way that leads to life.' So they do not live according to their own wills, nor obey their own desires and

pleasures, but behaving in accordance with the rule and judgement of another they live in monasteries and desire to have an Abbot ruling over them. Without doubt such men imitate the mind of the Lord in his saying, 'I came not to do my own will, but the will of him who sent me.'[36]

To help them in the quest to "present their bodies as a living sacrifice," Benedict gives his sons and daughters a threefold vow of obedience, stability, and the conversion of life. These vows are their three crosses on the hillside. Through them Benedict's children take up their cross to follow the Lamb. Through obedience they learn to obey like a child. Through stability they learn the simple trust of a child. Then through a lifetime of conversion they hope to finally become as little children and play forever in the court of the everlasting king.

Chapter Three Endnotes

1. Revelation 14:4, 7:17.

2. Abbot Parry (tr.), *The Rule of St. Benedict*, Leominster, Gracewing, 1997, p. 1.

3. Thomas N. Taylor (tr.), *Saint Thérèse of Lisieux, The Little Flower of Jesus*, New York, P. J. Kenedy, 1926, p. 232.

4. John Clarke, O.C.D. (tr.), *St. Thérèse of Lisieux: Her Last Conversations*, Washington, D.C., ICS Publications, 1977, p. 65.

5. John Saward, *The Way of the Lamb*, Edinburgh, T&T Clark, 1999, pp. 27-28.

6. Matthew 18:3.

7. Saward, p. 38.

8. Ibid.

9. Parry, p. 11.

10. Taylor, p. 295.

11. Ibid., p. 294.

12. Ibid.

13. John Clarke, O.C.D. (tr.), *General Correspondence, Vol. I*, Washington, D.C., ICS Publications, 1988, p. 510.

14. Letter to Mother Agnes, quoted in Saward, p. 25.

15. Clarke, *General Correspondence, Vol. II*, p. 724.

16. C. S. Lewis, *Miracles*, London, Fount, 1978, p. 78.

17. F. J. Sheed (tr.), *Collected Letters of Saint Thérèse of Lisieux*, London, Sheed and Ward, 1949, p. 241.

18. Ronald Knox (tr.), *Autobiography of a Saint*, London, Collins, 1973, p. 44.

19. Isaiah 66:12-13.

20. Hans Urs Von Balthasar, *Two Sisters in the Spirit*, San Francisco, Ignatius Press, 1970, pp. 118-119.

21. Saward, p. 39.

22. John Clarke, O.C.D. (tr.), *The Story of a Soul: The Autobiography of St. Thérèse of Lisieux*, Washington, D.C., ICS Publications, 1976, p. 136.

23. Knox, pp. 187-188.

24. Balthasar, p. 291.

25. Patrick Hart and Jonathan Montaldo (eds.), *The Intimate Merton*, Oxford, Lion, 1999, p. 51.

26. Clarke, *General Correspondence, Vol. II*, p. 909.

27. Knox, p. 215.

28. Saward, p. 144.

29. Aidan Nichols, O.P., *Christendom Awake*, Edinburgh, T&T Clark, 1999, pp.155-156.

30. Knox, p. 84.

31. Clarke, *The Story of a Soul*, p. 149.

32. Clarke, *[St. Thérèse's] Last Conversations*, p. 150.

33. Balthasar, p. 307.

34. Knox, p. 187.

35. Cf. Romans 12:1-2.

36. Parry, pp. 21-22.

Four

Childhood
and Obedience

Thoughts and Prayers

Have this mind among yourselves, which was in Christ Jesus, who, though he was in the form of God, did not count equality with God a thing to be grasped, but emptied himself, taking the form of a servant, being born in the likeness of men. And being found in human form he humbled himself and became obedient unto death, even death on a cross.

— Philippians 2:5-8

Having purified your souls by your obedience to the truth for a sincere love of the brethren, love one another earnestly from the heart.

— 1 Peter 1:22

It is so difficult to believe because it is so difficult to obey.

— Kierkegaard

The monastic experience asks you to say, write, and do things not differently but the same. It asks you to be obedient to age long traditions and to form your mind and heart according to often proved and approved principles.

— Henri Nouwen

The hard work of obedience happens in relationships.

— Columba Stewart, O.S.B.

Prayer
Take my hands and let them move at the impulse of Thy love.

— Francis Havergal

When a friend of Chesterton's read about the simplicity of God in Thomas Aquinas, she remarked, "Well, if that's His simplicity, I wonder what His complexity is like."[1] When Aquinas said God was simple, he meant God was whole and consistent, not incomplete or contradictory. The littlest child is simple in a similar way. It is not long before he becomes not only complicated but cantankerous; but at the earliest stage a child is simple as nature is simple. One fruit of a child's simplicity is that he obeys his parents with natural enthusiasm. He looks for ways to please and is delighted with little tasks and chores. His obedience is natural and free. He obeys because he wants to, not because he has to.

What is remarkable is that when things are as they should be, they are unremarkable. No one exclaims with delight when the train runs on time, or when the sun comes up each morning. Likewise, because the small child's obedience is natural it draws no attention to itself. We're surprised when the child starts to disobey, and after the initial surprise we are alarmed. We're not alarmed simply because the disobedience displeases us; we are alarmed because we suddenly realize that the disobedience is unnatural. A kink has appeared in our straightforward child. Something good has been twisted. In Eden, Adam and Eve lived like children in a state of innocent obedience, which was as natural as water running downhill or a rooster crowing at sunrise. When they disobeyed, their perception was altered, and therefore everything was altered. The shocking truth of the story is that disobedience not only twists our whole nature, but the whole of Nature.

Obedience is part of innocence; so if one wishes to learn the little way of spiritual childhood, it means relearning the simple obedience of the littlest child. As cynical grown-ups, not only do we find it impossible to obey, but we find it impossible to conceive of obedience as a virtue. To obey we must have someone to obey, yet we have been taught to distrust all authority, to search for the facts, and to make up our own mind. Science, scholarship, and cynicism have undermined one authority structure after another, so the only infallible statement left is that there are no infallible statements. Ironically, in rejecting an external infallible authority we are encouraged to embrace the most fickle and fallible of all authorities — our own judgment. We then cling to our opinions like a shipwrecked man clings to a splinter of wood, and, before long, our opinions are unassailable. In the end we don't have one objective, infallible authority but millions of subjective "infallible" authorities, and in this absurdity we rejoice.

In such a world the suggestion of obedience is met with incomprehension. That one should submit one's entire will to another individual is not only a social error but an antisocial horror. Obedience is a blasphemy in a world of individual freedom, and yet all the wise ones tell us it is only through obedience that innocence is recovered and retained. Obedience can only be rediscovered through discipline and commitment. Therefore Benedict sets obedience as one of the three vows for his monks. In his chapter on receiving brethren he writes, "The one who is to be accepted into the community must promise in the oratory, in the presence of all, stability, conversion of life and obedience."[2]

Like all natural gifts, obedience has to be practiced to be made perfect. This perfection requires a structure, a good teacher, and hard work. To practice obedience one has to get into the habit of obeying instantly. Benedict commends those who "at once leave whatever they are engaged on, abandon their own will, and with hands set free by leaving unfinished what they are doing, with the quick feet of obedience follow by action the voice of him who gives the order."[3] In practical terms it means, "as soon as the signal for the Divine Office is heard, the brethren must leave whatever they have been engaged in doing and hasten with all speed."[4] There is evidence from medieval manuscripts that the monks stopped their copying even in the middle of a word to get up and attend prayers. Thérèse did the same thing. She loved reading, but says, "I made it a point of duty to break off promptly at the end of the time allotted, even in the middle of the most interesting passage."[5] Like the monks, she obeyed her rule literally; so in a letter to her sister she writes, "I must leave you, nine o'clock is stri—"[6]

Benedict's obedience is military in its strictness, and it is no coincidence that both he and Thérèse see the spiritual life as warfare. They agree with St. Paul that "we are not contending against flesh and blood, . . . but against the spiritual hosts of wickedness in the heavenly places."[7] From his call to arms in the Prologue, Benedict links the monk's vow of obedience to his status as a soldier of Christ. Like a general of Byzantium standing against the invading Hun Benedict says, "My words are addressed to you, who by giving up your own will, are taking up the strong and glorious weapons of obedience in order to do battle in the service of the Lord Christ, the True King."[8]

For those who have only known her as "the little flower," the militant spirit of Thérèse is the most surprising element of her teaching. Thérèse wrote poems and plays in honor of Joan of Arc. A serendipitous photograph shows her dressed in armor to perform the part of Joan in one of her plays. Echoing the Virgin Mary and St. Paul, and with a romantic zeal for battle, Thérèse proclaims her mission: "I have put on the breastplate of the Almighty, and he has armed me with the strength of his arms. Henceforth no terror can wound me, for who can now divide me from his love? By his side, I advance to the battlefield, fearing neither fire nor steel; my enemies shall discover that I am a queen and the bride of a King."[9]

This little flower is no shrinking violet. She is a spiritual swashbuckler, a female chevalier, and a crusading knight . She declares, "God has granted me the grace of being totally un-afraid of war; I must do my duty, whatever the cost."[10] "Let us fight without ceasing, even without hope of winning the battle for what does success matter! Let us keep going, however ex-hausting the struggle may be."[11] Elsewhere she says, "I long to accomplish the most heroic deeds, I feel within me the courage of the crusader. I would die on the battlefield in defence of the Church!"[12] On her deathbed, like a spiritual Cyrano de Bergerac, she says, "I shall die with weapons in hand!"[13] Balthasar points out that the terrible weapons she has in mind are her absolute poverty, virginity, and obedience.[14] In this she echoes Benedict, who also calls obedience a weapon.

To speak romantically of spiritual warfare seems quaint and somehow distasteful to those who will do anything for a peaceful life. War has never been a romantic crusade, but modern war is especially hellish. In opposing war, we mustn't conclude that there is nothing worth fighting for. Benedict and Thérèse's militant spirit reminds us that there are not only things worth fighting for but also things worth dying for. When examined, our antipathy to-ward battle may be the same thing as our antipathy toward life. It is a kind of terminal cowardice that is not so much pacifist, but passive. The frightening corollary of our passivity is that if we have nothing to die for, we also have nothing to live for. In con-trast, Benedict and Thérèse are thrilled by the prospect of battle and are willing to risk everything to win the spiritual war. They speak of war and weapons because they believe, like their Lord, that eternal life is worth dying for. Indeed, dying is the only way to attain eternal life, and if that is so, what better way to die, than in battle? As a result Benedict spurs his monks on to be good soldiers of Christ, and Thérèse says to her novices, "I always want to see you behaving like a brave soldier who does not complain about his own suffering but takes his comrades' wounds seriously and treats his own as nothing but scratches."[15]

Obedience is a weapon against evil because through obedience the selfish will is broken, and a crack in Satan's battlements appears. This is why to obey the superior in the monastery is the first step in obedience to Christ. Benedict says:

> The first step in humility is prompt obedience . . . immediately when something has been commanded by a superior, it is for them [the monks] as a divine command and they cannot allow any delay in its execution . . . for the obedience that is shown to superiors is shown to God; for he said himself, 'He who listens to you listens to me.'[16]

Since obedience is the first and most valuable weapon in the war, Benedict's monks "do not live according to their own wills, nor obey their own desires and pleasures, but behaving in accordance with the rule and judgement of another, they live in monasteries and desire to have an Abbot ruling over them."[17]

The monks or nuns in their monastery are like soldiers camped on the front line. They are trained in obedience and ready for action against the enemy. Benedict contrasts this with the rebellious monks called Sarabaites. In chapter one he describes them:

> They have not been tested by a rule, as gold is tested in a furnace, nor been taught by experience, but are like soft lead. They keep faith with this world by their actions. These people have no shepherd, they shut themselves up in their own sheepfolds, not those of the Lord; and their law consists in yielding to their desires: what they like or

choose they call holy, and they reckon illicit whatever displeases them.[18]

Benedict's words describe not only cantankerous monks, but
every sort of do-it-yourself Christian. Benedict is clear that
homemade churches are wrong. They are "sheepfolds of their
own making." The same attitude applies to any Christian who
thinks he can interpret the Bible or decide on moral questions
without any higher authority. If left to ourselves, we will inevi-
tably choose what seems right to us; but as the writer of Proverbs says, "There is a way that seems right to a man which leads
only to destruction."[19]

Benedict's diatribe against Sarabaites chokes the natural
desire to chase after individual "freedom." The search for freedom is good, but too often it leaves us jaded and enslaved by a
cohort of elusive desires. By contrast, anyone who submits to a
higher discipline soon discovers a new kind of freedom. Thérèse
delights in the freedom that comes through a vow of obedience:

> How much anxiety we are spared through taking the
> vow of obedience! How happy are the simple religious!
> Their sole compass being the will of their superiors, they
> are always certain of being on the right road; they have no
> fear of being mistaken even when it seems that their supe-
> riors are wrong.[20]

Religious obedience may seem a simple route to freedom,
but it is full of pitfalls. Some people embrace religious obedience as an escape from the demands of life. The religious life
provides a meal ticket, and obedience seems a small price to pay
for the luxury of being looked after. Some seek freedom without

responsibility; this person seeks slavery because it frees him from responsibility. One who seeks obedience under those terms sells one's soul just as diabolically as the one who sells his soul for pleasures that are more obviously irresponsible. When Thérèse talks about the freedom of obedience, she is referring to something far more mysterious and profound. Those who seek obedience out of a desire to opt out of life will change their minds as soon as obedience becomes difficult. Thérèse stands this natural instinct on its head. She thinks there is freedom in obeying even when the superior seems wrong. Time and again Thérèse obeyed when the command seemed ill-judged or even absurd. In her last illness when the infirmarian suggested she take a short walk, each day Thérèse did so, even though the walk exhausted her and made her condition worse. Benedict advises:

> When in the very act of obeying one meets with trials, opposition and even abuse, a man should, with an uncomplaining spirit, keep a firm grip on patience and as he endures he should neither grow faint nor run away; even as Scripture says, 'He who stands firm to the end will be saved,' . . . these are the trials through which we triumph on account of him who has loved us.[21]

Struggling to obey a difficult command is one thing, but what should be done if a superior makes an order that is not only difficult but absurd? If the order is absurd, then the act of obedience becomes absurd as well. Thérèse answers absurdity with absurdity: "There is no merit in doing what is reasonable,"[22] she says. What better illustration of absurd obedience than the story of Father Abraham being ordered to take his son Isaac up Mount Moriah to be sacrificed?[23] For years he had waited for a child to be born. Finally in his old age he is given a son. Then

God commands him to kill the son. Nevertheless, Abraham is quick to obey. What Abraham couldn't see is how his absurd act of obedience rippled down through time. Two thousand years later, when God's only Son carried the wood of his own sacrifice up the mountain of Golgotha, the absurd obedience of Abraham suddenly made sense.

Benedict and Thérèse sense the possibility that obedience can become absurd. Nevertheless, they do not flinch from the call to obedience, because they also sense that the absurd is often absurdly meaningful. Abraham's obedience to an absurd command eventually made sense; but Benedict and Thérèse know that even if the command never becomes clear, there is still virtue in obedience because through obedience self-will is broken. The breaking of self-will becomes the meaning, redeeming the absurdity and making the absurd meaningful. Benedict says:

> A man should not love his own will nor take pleasure in carrying out his desires, but rather by his actions imitate the Lord in saying, 'I came not to do my own will, but that of him who sent me' . . . for the love of God one should be obedient to a superior in all things, imitating the Lord of whom the Apostle says, 'He was made obedient even unto death.'[24]

What could be more absurd than the cross, where the King of Creation dies as a small-time criminal in a provincial town? Yet the cross is the everlasting example of the absurd obedience that brings redemption. Chesterton was right when he said, "I have seen the Truth and it doesn't make any sense."[25] The foolishness of God is wiser than the wisdom of men.

As any fool knows, there is freedom in absurdity. The freedom that Thérèse proclaims through absolute obedience is the

freedom to be oneself. Even in absurd obedience — especially
in absurd obedience — self-will is broken, and with it the grown-
up immaturity that always demands a logical answer. When that
freedom breaks open, the soul finds her proper place within the
Father's will. She is free to live without knowing the meaning of
everything because she lives within the One who is the Meaning and the Everything. To live in the Father's will is to be in the
place where one was created to be. At that point the real person
begins to live for the first time. This profound freedom is hidden in the story of the prodigal son. When the son is in the
pigpen, the New Testament says that "he came to himself."[26] It
was at that point that he decided to obey. The freedom Thérèse
offers is the freedom to "come to ourselves," to be who we were
created to be, to find our rightful place in the cosmos; to live in
harmony with the Creator, and "to find our peace in His will."[27]

Freedom through obedience is well illustrated by the genius
and discipline of music. A talented pianist must practice from
childhood if he wishes to play a masterpiece like Rachmaninoff's
Third Piano Concerto. For years the novice does his scales, attends his music lessons, and obediently plays a series of dull and
uncongenial pieces. He obeys his teacher and the master who
composed the score. At times the practice is routine; at other
times it is impossibly difficult. He feels like giving up. He ar-
gues with his teacher; but if he perseveres, one day he steps
onstage and plays the Rachmaninoff concerto with utter confidence, panache, and exhilarating freedom. Furthermore, he makes
the whole thing look easy. His genius has been set free and the
result is an astounding act of inspiration, beauty, and power. In
hindsight, not only has he soared with power and life as he played
the concerto, but the final perfection has made every moment of
drudgery enjoyable as well. At that moment of freedom he has
become all that he was created to be, and the beauty, power, and

climax of the piece is woven from each moment of discipline, hard work, and obedience that took him to that achievement.

Obedience promises freedom, but there is a huge risk because obedience also threatens the most odious form of slavery. Religious people have an unfortunate taste for Pharisaism, and the call to obedience attracts two kinds of Pharisees — those who love to dominate and those who love to be dominated. Within religion the two personality types attract each other like some symbiotic sinister disease. The one who dominates and the one who wishes to be dominated collude to construct a religion that gives a twisted pleasure to both. Even worse, once they have sealed their alliance they work together to draw others into the web. Together the Pharisaical parasites feed off the guilt and insecurity of others. With threats, promises, and false friendship they draw weak souls to the worst kind of destruction — religious fanaticism and spiritual pride based on fear. Jesus Christ hardly condemned anyone, but these are the ones he called a brood of serpents and sons of Satan.

The one who spiritually dominates and abuses others is too often aided by the one who wishes to be dominated. In the spiritual life the person who is acquiescent may look perfectly obedient, but it is possible such a person has not yet begun the journey. Maybe such persons have chosen Quietism — that heresy which believes obedience is a passive choice; that the soul obeys like a leaf in the wind. If so, their obedience is mere acquiescence. They have not controlled their will; rather, they have killed it. The kind of obedience Thérèse and Benedict call for is an active obedience, an obedience that struggles to obey because it is struggling to conquer self-will.

Benedict expects instant obedience from his monks, but he does not expect them to be mindless clones. They are to struggle with obedience. They will not get the blessing unless they first wrestle with the angel, and even so, they may emerge from the battle blessed but wounded. That's why obedience for Benedict and Thérèse is so intimately bound up with being a soldier of Christ. As warriors they must battle both with the devil and with themselves. The struggle to obey is the spiritual struggle par excellence. It is within that struggle that grace is given and spiritual power flows.

Thérèse struggled with obedience. She was told she could not enter the convent at the age of fifteen. She submitted to authority, but she also challenged the authority. She convinced her father to change his mind, then she convinced the bishop to change his mind. She even asked the Pope personally to bend the rules. Benedict makes provision for the monk to question the authority and challenge commands he thinks are wrong.

> If it should happen that burdensome or impossible tasks are imposed on one of the brethren he should indeed accept with complete calm and obedience the command of the one who so orders, but if he sees that the weight of the burden quite exceeds the limits of his strength, he should quietly and at a suitable moment explain to his superior the reasons why he cannot do it.[28]

Obedience is still required, but Benedict expects his monks to struggle with the commandments.

By its very nature obedience must be difficult, and those who do not struggle with obedience have not begun to obey. Those who will not struggle believe obedience means constantly obeying the rules without question; but if they do not ask questions they will never have the answers. They have chosen the path of least resistance, and think avoiding battle is the same thing as winning the war. Although they may obey all the rules they are spiritually asleep. Benedict tries to rouse them: "Now is the hour for us to rise from sleep. Let us, then, open our eyes to the divine light and hear with our ears the divine voice as it cries out to us daily."[29] From the front line Thérèse wakes them with her battle cry. "Sanctity!" she cries. "It must be won at the point of a sword."[30]

The struggle to obey is the struggle of rebellion, repentance, and return, which is crucial for the soul's salvation. Two sets of sons show the different attitudes. In the story of the prodigal son, one son struggles with obedience. He rebels, repents, and returns. The second son looks obedient, but by the end of the story he had not yet begun to fight, and so he had not fully obeyed. Jesus tells another story about two sons. The father asks both of them to work in the fields. One says he will go and does not. The second says he will not, but goes. The first doubtless planned to fulfill his promise later on, and so thought he was being obedient while he never was. The second struggled with obedience and won the day.

The religious person who dominates others and the one who colludes with him are both guilty of legalism. One loves to impose the law because it makes him feel strong; the other loves to have it imposed because it makes him feel safe. The terrifying realization for anyone who is the least bit religious is that each one of us is inclined to drift into one category or the other. Either we seek a religious master to dominate our will or we seek to control the will of others. In each case we substitute authentic authority for authoritarianism and paralyzing fear for perfect love. Both the spiritual dominator and the dominated prefer the fear they know to the love they do not know. Although it is easy to be hard on those who love legalism, they deserve pity, not blame, for legalism is, at heart, a form of fear.

The answer to this twisted authoritarianism is not anarchy but mutual submission in love. The superior must teach in all sincerity in both word and action. Benedict says the abbot should "rule over his disciples with two kinds of teaching; that is to say, he must show forth all good and holy things by his words and even more by his deeds."[31] If the monk is to obey the abbot, the abbot must also submit in a loving way to his sons by adapting himself to their needs. The abbot "must realize how difficult and arduous is the task he has undertaken, that of ruling souls and serving men of many different characters. . . . Thus he must adapt and fit himself to all."[32]

Thérèse had her mother superior. Benedict's monks have their abbot. If we are not monks or nuns, whom do we obey? First, we obey God's natural law, living as naturally as possible in an unnatural technological society. Second, we obey the circumstances of our life, which we have no power to change. Third, we submit to the teachings of Christ's Church. Fourth, if true obedience is love in action, then we obey those with whom we live by loving them in all our words and works. Benedict and Thérèse's little way cannot be lived in isolation. Obedience is always set in the context of community. Those who are obedient in love first learn to obey their superior, and once they have learned to obey him they soon want to "obey" everyone they meet.

Benedict recognizes that for the innocent heart obedience extends beyond the abbot to embrace everyone: "The goodness of obedience should be shown not only . . . to the Abbot, but the brethren should also obey each other in the knowledge that by this path of obedience they will draw nearer to God."[33] The truly obedient monk no longer obeys his father abbot and brother monks out of a sense of discipline, but out of a sincere desire. He has become like the littlest child who obeys because he wants to, and he wants to because his love is pure.

To be obedient is to reach out actively and naturally to do unto others before they know that they should do anything for us. Within marriage it means wives obeying their husbands because the husbands have first obeyed their wives by loving them in a totally self-sacrificial way.[34] In the workplace it means listening to the needs of others and providing service and a smile even when others are being difficult. In the home it means children obeying parents because the parents have first "obeyed" the children by sacrificing their time, money, and lives for the children's welfare.

Obedience is not only seeking to do unto others what we would have them do to us, but it also means putting up with others as we would have them put up with us. Benedict says, "They should with the greatest patience make allowance for one another's weaknesses, whether physical or moral."[35] The root of the word "obey" means "to listen," so patient attention to others is part of obedience. In an enclosed monastery, life becomes focused and small annoyances loom large; obeying others may simply mean putting up with them. As in any home, the minor irritations often require more heroics to endure than the great tests of sanctity. Thérèse records her struggle with a sister who splashes her with water thoughtlessly, and her trial of patience with another sister who clatters her rosary beads:

> At prayer I was for a long time near a sister who used to handle incessantly either her rosary beads or some other thing. . . . I cannot say how it tormented me! I should have liked to turn my head and look at the culprit so as to make her stop that noise: however in my heart I knew it was better to bear it patiently. . . . I kept quiet therefore, but was sometimes worked up to fever heat and obliged to make simply a prayer of endurance.[36]

Benedict and Thérèse's service to others is an imitation of Christ who "came not to be served, but to serve, and to give his life as a ransom for many." In service to others Christ is imitated, but he is also served, for in serving others we serve Christ in them. Thus submitting to others in service is a way of obeying Christ himself.[37] Benedict makes this clear in his advice on the reception of guests: "All who arrive as guests are to be welcomed like Christ, for he is going to say, 'I was a stranger and you welcomed me.' "[38] Likewise, Benedict reminds the monks that in serving the sick they are serving Christ.[39]

Thérèse takes this principle even further. She wants to obey Christ not only in the stranger and the guest, and not only in her sisters in the convent, but in those she finds most difficult to love. She describes how there was one sister who "had a genius" for displeasing her in everything she did. Thérèse says:

> So I set about doing everything for this Sister that I would have done for the person I loved most. Each time I met her, I prayed to God for her, offering him all her virtues and merits. I felt that this was pleasing to Jesus, for there is no artist who does not like to receive praise for his works, and Jesus, artist of souls, is happy when we do not stop at the exterior but penetrate to the inner sanctuary where he has chosen to dwell and admire its beauty. Ah! What attracted me was Jesus hidden in the depths of her soul.[40]

Balthasar observes, "The person in whom Jesus dwells is like the veil bearing the marks of his face; the two aspects are inseparable, and whoever loves the one must, like Thérèse, love the whole person."[41]

The summary of obedience is the Life of Love. In obedience to others we lose ourselves and find Christ, and as we love him we begin to love and obey our brothers and sisters in him. Thérèse expresses it fully: "Remembering that charity covers a multitude of sins, I draw from this rich mine that Jesus has opened up before me. 'I have run in the way of your commandments since you have enlarged my heart.' Only charity can expand my heart."[42]

In other words, only Love can enable Thérèse to obey God and her neighbor. In her desire to "run in the way of God's commandments" Thérèse unconsciously echoes Benedict, for in his Prologue he alludes to the same psalm. With sparkling vigor he calls his monks to the same joyful obedience, challenging them to run with him "in the path of God's commandments — our hearts overflowing with the inexpressible delight of love."[43]

Chapter Four Endnotes

1. G. K. Chesterton, *St. Thomas Aquinas*, London, Hodder and Stoughton, 1943, p. x.
2. Abbot Parry (tr.), *The Rule of St. Benedict*, Leominster, Gracewing, 1997, p. 94.
3. Ibid., p. 21.
4. Ibid., p. 71.
5. John Clarke, O.C.D. (tr.); *The Story of a Soul: The Autobiography of St. Thérèse of Lisieux*, Washington, D.C., ICS Publications, 1976, p. 71.
6. John Clarke, O.C.D. (tr.), *General Correspondence, Vol. I*, Washington, D.C., ICS Publications, 1988, p. 427.
7. Ephesians 6:12.
8. Parry, p. 1.
9. From a poem by Thérèse, quoted in Hans Urs Von Balthasar, *Two Sisters in the Spirit*, San Francisco, Ignatius Press, 1970, p. 151.
10. Clarke, *The Story of a Soul*, p. 240.
11. Thomas N. Taylor (tr.), *Saint Thérèse of Lisieux, The Little Flower of Jesus*, New York, P. J. Kenedy, 1926, p. 324.
12. Clarke, *The Story of a Soul*, p. 187.
13. John Clarke, O.C.D. (tr.), *St. Thérèse of Lisieux: Her Last Conversations*, Washington, D.C., ICS Publications, 1977, p. 237.

14. Balthasar, p. 239.
15. Taylor, p. 303.
16. Parry, p. 21.
17. Ibid.
18. Ibid., p. 7.
19. Proverbs 16:25.
20. Clarke, *The Story of a Soul*, pp. 218-219.
21. Parry, p. 26.
22. Taylor, p. 294.
23. Cf. Genesis 22.
24. Parry, p. 26.
25. Cf. 1 Corinthians 1:25.
26. Cf. Luke 15:17.
27. Dorothy L. Sayers and Barbara Reynolds (tr.), *Paradiso*, London, Penguin, 1976, iii.85.
28. Parry, p. 112.
29. Ibid., p. 1.
30. Clarke, *General Correspondence, Vol. I*, p. 558.
31. Parry, p. 12.
32. Ibid., p. 13.
33. Ibid., p. 115.
34. Cf. Ephesians 5:22, 25.
35. Parry, p. 116.
36. Ronald Knox (tr.), *Autobiography of a Saint*, London, Collins, 1973, pp. 236-237.
37. Cf. Matthew 25:40.
38. Parry, p. 83.
39. Ibid., p. 64.
40. Clarke, *The Story of a Soul*, p. 222.
41. Balthasar, p. 169.
42. Clarke, *The Story of a Soul*, pp. 224-226.
43. Parry, p. 4.

Five

Childhood
and Stability

Thoughts and Prayers

He only is my rock and my salvation, / my fortress; I shall not be shaken.

— PSALM 62:6

Every one then who hears these words of mine and does them will be like a wise man who built his house upon the rock; and the rain fell, and the floods came, and the winds blew and beat upon that house, but it did not fall, because it had been founded on the rock.

— MATTHEW 7:24-25

The meaning of stability: God is not elsewhere.
God is nearer to me than I am to myself; He is just as near to wood and stone, but they do not know it.

— MEISTER ECKHART

Stability says there must be no evasion; instead attend to the real.

— ESTHER DEWAAL

Go, sit in your cell, and your cell will teach you everything.

— ABBOT MOSES OF SCETE

Prayer
Thou Who hast prepared a place for my soul;
Prepare my soul for that place.

— JOSEPH HALL

St. Augustine spoke for every grown-up when he prayed, "O God, You have created us for Yourself and our hearts are restless 'til they find their rest in You." In contrast to the restless grown-up, the innocent child, playing and singing a little song, is caught up in his game. He is unaware of time, unaware of himself, unaware of stress, worry, or fear. He radiates a natural calm. He is stable and totally free. Such unselfconscious innocence soon dies and restlessness runs riot where stability once stood.

The child's innocent stability is based on his perceived security. In a loving home his needs are provided before he asks. Ideally, two parents surround him with an unconditional love that covers a multitude of fears. Secure in the love of God the Father and in the embrace of Mother Church, those who follow the little way of spiritual childhood have learned to live in this same natural stability and peace. Benedict believes stability is so important that he makes it one of the three monastic vows: "The one who is to be accepted into the community must promise in the oratory, in the presence of all, stability, conversion of life and obedience."[1]

The monk's vow of stability is intimately linked with his vow of obedience. When the monk submits to his superior, he fulfills his vow of obedience. When he submits to his particular environment and set of circumstances, he fulfills his vow of stability. With the psalmist, Benedict's monks sing, "My heart is fixed, O Lord, my heart is fixed." The monk's vow of stability is fulfilled in his lifetime commitment to his community. Benedict puts this fact in a stark way at the end of his chapter on receiving brethren. After the monk takes his solemn vows, "From that day onwards he is to be reckoned among the community."[2] He has accepted a life sentence. He is married to that community and they to him for better or for worse, for richer or for poorer, in sickness and in health, until death do them part.

As always, Benedict sees the physical and the spiritual as intertwined. The monk's physical commitment to a particular monastery is linked with his spiritual stability. He cannot have one without the other. Benedict contrasts the rootedness of the cenobite — the community-based monk — with those monastic mavericks he calls "gyrovagues." The gyrovagues, it is pointed out, "are never stable their whole lives, but wanderers through diverse regions, receiving hospitality in the monastic cells of others for three or four days at a time. Always roving and never settling, they follow their own wills, enslaved by the attractions of gluttony."[3]

Benedict paints a vivid portrait of the bored soul. He is a spiritual channel hopper, always looking for the next stimulus, the next religious entertainment, the next spiritual thrill. Benedict would not reserve his condemnation for discontented monks. Church-shopping is one of the spiritual diseases of our age. Constantly on the lookout for an excellent preacher, good music, fine liturgy, or pleasing architecture, we become liturgical tasters and our taste becomes so refined that, like the connoisseur who has spoiled his appreciation through snobbery, we can never find a church exquisite enough for us.

Benedict sees a spiritual disease underneath this physical restlessness. The disease is discontent, and it is caused by disobedience. We are born with the instinct to be our own masters; we imagine all authority to be authoritarian and do everything to avoid its claims over us. We even imagine our restless disobedience to be romantic and sophisticated. We see ourselves as brave individuals or intrepid spiritual explorers — one of those courageous souls who always seek but never find. We swallow seductive aphorisms like, "It is better to travel honestly than to arrive," forgetting the obvious fact that traveling without a destination is the same thing as being lost.

Certainly we must search for God, but we need discipline

and guidance to ensure we are running on the right path, not just running in circles. Our capacity for self-deception is so great that it is very possible to imagine we are searching for God when, in fact, we are fleeing from him with all our energy. Without stability and a superior authority we are more likely to find a god of our own making than the God who made us. We need to settle down and center down. The vow of stability is the discipline that ensures we are pilgrims and not fugitives. Benedict says: Commit yourself. Make a vow of stability and find reality, even if the reality is grim.

At the heart of our restlessness is our fear of being alone with God and alone with ourselves. The spiritual life is essentially one of being alone, and the word "monk" comes from the Greek *monos*, or "alone." Benedict says the ideal monk is the hermit. Hermits are the ones who "have been tested for a long time in the monastery and have learnt, with the assistance of many brothers, how to do battle against the devil, and now . . . they are strong enough to do battle . . . on their own with their own resources relying on God's aid, by now without the support of anyone else."[4]

The hermit reminds the world of the Gospel call that unless we leave father and mother and brother and sister for the sake of Christ, we cannot enter the kingdom. Thérèse understood the need for this solitude. Although she was in a convent with her beloved older sisters, she deliberately refused to seek them out for either pleasant conversation or spiritual consolation. Thérèse knew the way of sanctity could only be walked alone. At the end she was surrounded by well-wishers but realized that not even the closest sister truly understood her strange and terrible calling. Her solitary path is a reminder that the spiritual life brings each of us face to face with God alone, and we cannot do this without first coming face to face with ourselves alone.

If I am frightened of solitude, it is not because I am frightened of being alone, but because I am frightened of the person who will be there with me; and that frightening person is myself. All the spiritual masters have understood that to make progress we must first, like the prodigal, "come to our self." For the monk, this demand to face oneself is tied to solitude and that solitude is linked to the monk's physical bondage to the monastery and to his cell. Thomas Merton recalls one of the stories of the Desert Fathers: "A certain brother went to Abbot Moses in Scete, and asked him for a good word. And the elder said to him: Go, sit in your cell, and your cell will teach you everything."[5]

For the Desert Fathers, their cell was often a cave. In his first monastic trial Benedict lived in a cave at Subiaco, and Thérèse was filled with quiet joy when she first set eyes on her barren cell in Carmel.[6] The cave cell is a powerful image for the dark, solitary confinement that is part of the vow of stability. The monk intentionally enters a place of sensory deprivation. He turns his back on all the vapid entertainment and flashy enticements of the world. He does so not because he is a spoilsport, but because he is drawn to something infinitely more beautiful and terrifying. The cave is his prodigal's pigpen where he confronts the mud from which he was made. In the cave he goes down to the underworld of his own soul. He goes there to find a hidden treasure, and the treasure he goes to find is the little child who was buried by the grown-up he has become.

The inner landscape is vast and dark. Chaos reigns, and sometimes no sign of life or sense can be found. When we are faced with the darkness within, all seems confusing and we can only walk by faith. We can only trust that God is helping us recover the treasure and is leading us back to the land of light. Thérèse spoke vividly of the same dark underworld:

> Jesus took me by the hand and brought me into a sub-
> terranean way, where it was neither hot nor cold, where the
> sun does not shine, and rain and wind do not come; a tunnel
> where I see nothing but a brightness half-veiled. . . . I do
> not see that we are advancing towards the mountain that is
> our goal, because our journey is under the earth; yet I have a
> feeling that we are approaching it, without knowing why.[7]

The journey into solitary darkness is often the result of the
vow of stability. Life has become so small, so enclosed, and the
vision has become so narrowed, that there is nowhere else to
look but up. While stability forces the inner journey, it also enables it. Without the security stability provides, the inner journey would be impossible. Because Thérèse has utter security in
her stable monastic life, her courageous inner journey has outward support. She sums it up with the image of a tree stretching
for the light:

> In the religious life, the soul, like the young oak, is
> hemmed in on all sides by its Rule. All its movements are
> hampered, interfered with by the other trees . . . but it has
> light when it looks toward heaven, there alone it can rest
> its gaze, never upon anything below; it need not be afraid
> of rising too high.[8]

Stability is also linked with detachment. Benedict wisely
links the gyrovague's restlessness with gluttony, and one of the
key reasons for our restlessness is greed. Some people are coarsely
greedy, but for most people acquisitiveness is really a desire for
security. We accumulate more of everything in order to keep the
wolves of future insecurity from the door. Benedict follows the
Gospel in saying this form of materialism is a false god. If we

are looking to material things for our peace, we will have neither material satisfaction nor inner peace.

Because restlessness is linked with greed, Benedict links stability with poverty. In his instructions for receiving brothers, just after the monk makes his vow to seek stability of life Benedict says, "If he has any possessions, he must either previously give them to the poor, or by means of formal donation give them to the monastery, keeping for himself nothing at all."[9] In a powerful paradox Benedict makes the monk promise stability at the same moment that he gives away all those things on which most people base their stability. Benedict's severity continues: "No one may take it upon himself to give or receive anything without the Abbot's permission, or to possess as his own anything whatever, books or writing tablets or pen or anything at all . . . they must expect to receive everything they need from the Father of the monastery."[10] Neither may the monk receive letters or gifts from outside the monastery. "Everything should be common to all."[11]

That all his needs are provided by the abbot points the monk back to his utter dependence on God, for everything he has, including his own life, has been lent to him by God, and he is to be a good steward of the gifts he has been given. Benedict also weaves these lessons into his instructions for the cellarer (that is, the senior monk who administers and distributes the material things of the monastery): "He must keep under his own care whatever the Abbot has entrusted to him . . . knowing for certain that he will have to render account for his treatment of them all."[12] Because in the divine economy all things belong to everyone, each person is only lent material things for proper use:

> With regard to the monastery's material possessions
> such as tools, clothes, or other articles, the Abbot should

put in charge of them brethren whose way of life and character he can trust, and then commit all these things to them as he thinks best, for safe keeping and return after use.[13]

Thérèse is similarly detached from material things: "Jesus does not want me to lay claim to what belongs to me. This ought to seem easy and natural to me, since nothing is mine. I have renounced the goods of this earth through the vow of poverty."[14]

The strict denial of material possessions helps the monk be detached from material things in order to depend on God alone. Benedict knows that until the monk is detached from personal possessions, the niggling restlessness and desire that accompany greed will always be there, and that restless desire is the enemy of true stability.

Thérèse also realizes that stability and security are not provided by material things. She recounts her disappointment in an avenue of chestnut trees. It was springtime and she had gone to enjoy the beauties of nature. "I so loved the shadows cast by the branches, and there were none that year. The branches, already green, were lying in bundles on the ground, and all that remained were the trunks of the trees."[15]

Her disappointment makes her realize true peace is found in God alone: "I will fret no more about transitory things; my Well-Beloved shall take the place of all else for me."[16] In a letter to her sister she sums it up, "In this world we must not become attached to anything — not even things the most innocent, for they fail us at the moment when we are least expecting it. The eternal alone can satisfy us."[17] This realization brings Thérèse to praise the ground of her inner stability: "There is no stay, no support to seek outside of Jesus. He alone does not change. What happiness to think that he can never change!"[18]

In the second letter to the Corinthians St. Paul teaches, "We look for the things which are unseen, not the things which are seen, for the things which are unseen are eternal and the things which are seen are temporal."[19] Detachment from material things does not mean the material world is sinful, simply that it is passing. Benedict's strict Rule forbidding personal possessions is not a denial of the goodness of the physical world. He is no Manichee. While Benedict forbids personal possessions, he does not demand absolute poverty; neither does he say that possessions are evil. The community is allowed to own and administer all good things. Indeed, one of the marks of Benedict's wise Rule is his reverent treatment of physical things. He gives careful instructions on the brothers' food and drink, on their shoes and clothing. The tools and goods of the monastery are to be treated carefully — not just because they are expensive to replace, but because they have value in themselves. Indeed, the cellarer is to "regard the chattels of the monastery and its whole property as if they were the sacred vessels of the altar."[20] This careful attention to physical things is a sign of true detachment. The one who is indifferent disregards the physical. The one who is attached worships the physical. The one who is detached treats each thing with attention and care according to its own value. As Thomas Traherne has written, "Can you be righteous unless you be just in rendering to things their due esteem? All things were made to be yours and you were made to prize them according to their value."[21]

The religious is detached from personal possessions, and from human intimacy, and left on his own; but this kind of aloneness is far from the individualistic and romantic isolation of the artist. The monk is alone not because he is a unique genius, but because he is Everyman, and in his aloneness he is acknowledging each person's essential alienation from God, from others, and from his true self. The monk is a unique individual not because he is different from everyone else, but because he is the same as everyone else. He seems different because he is one of the few people who has recognized that he is *not* different. This aloneness binds us profoundly to the essential loneliness at the heart of every man. Thomas Merton has written:

> The solitary is one who is aware of solitude in himself as a basic and inevitable human reality, not just as something that affects him. Hence, his solitude is the foundation of a deep, pure and gentle sympathy with all other people, and the doorway by which he enters into the mystery of God and brings others into that mystery.[22]

To find stability means being detached from material possessions, but it also means being detached from our false self. Self isolates us from others and makes us feel different. As we are detached from self we come to realize how much we have in common with everyone else.

When Henri Nouwen visited a Trappist monastery for seven months, he was confronted with his desire to be different and therefore superior.

> I have always had a strange desire to be different than other people. . . . I wanted to say, write or do something 'different' or 'special' that would be noticed or talked about. . . . The monastic experience attacks this type of attention drawing. It asks you to say, write and do things not differently but the same. It asks you to be obedient to age long traditions . . . there is a remarkable avoidance of trying to be different, sensational and original. What this place is calling me to be is the same and more of the same.

The same as the monks, the same as the saints, the same
as Jesus, the same as the heavenly Father. The Rule of St.
Benedict, the returning rhythms of the day, the continu-
ous recitation of the psalms and the uniformity of dress,
food and place slowly make you aware of a powerful same-
ness that transcends time and place and unifies you with
the one God who is the Father of all people, all places and
all times, and who is the same through ages unending.[23]

Detachment is not the same thing as indifference. The ni-
hilist may achieve a certain peace of mind because he has become indifferent to the physical world, but this is nothing but
the placid face of resigned desperation. The stability that comes
from Christian detachment is a dynamic virtue. Christian detachment is based on hope, and that hope rests in the confidence of God the Father's dynamic love. Benedict describes the
stability of the person who has learned to be detached: "Everyone who listens to these words of mine and acts on them, will be
like the sensible man who built his house on rock; flood rose,
gales blew and hurled themselves against that house, and it did
not fall; it was founded on rock."[24]

Thérèse also knows the stability that comes with detachment
from physical things and attachment to God's love, but she takes
this detachment one stage further. Not content with utter poverty
and detachment from her closest loved ones, she even wishes to
be detached from her goodness. Like everything else, the grace
she has received from God is a gift that is lent to her for use and
return. "Since earthly goods do not belong to me, I should find no
difficulty in never reclaiming them when they are sometimes taken
away from me. The goods of heaven don't belong to me either;
they are lent to me by God."[25] In this she echoes Benedict, who
writes about the tools of good works, "If we make full use of them

unceasingly day and night, then, when we give them back on the Day of Judgement, we shall in return receive from the Lord that reward which he himself has promised."[26] For both Benedict and Thérèse their good works are simply tools lent to them by God. Thérèse realizes that everything, but especially her goodness, comes from God, and that her inner stability is built on her complete trust in God's grace. Speaking about those who will read her writings she says, "They will understand that everything comes from God; and what I shall have of glory from it will be a gratuitous gift from God that doesn't belong to me."[27]

The danger of detachment is that it can lead to rootlessness. To avoid this danger, detachment is interwoven with the vow of stability. Paradoxically, the spiritual person can only be truly detached if he is attached. In other words, he must remain rooted if he is to grow with complete freedom. To nurture the necessary rootedness, Benedict imposes stability of place. The monk vows to remain enclosed within one particular community, and that means one particular geographical location, one set of buildings, and one group of people. This commitment to one place produces the outer stability that eventually helps form an inner stability. Outward stability is not an end in itself; instead it helps create an environment in which the soul may prosper. So at the end of his chapter on the "tools of good works" Benedict says, "Now the workshop in which we make diligent use of all these tools is the enclosure of the monastery combined with the stability in the community."[28]

Detachment makes the monk realize that other things will not make him happy, and stability forces him to realize that other places will not make him happy either. Spiritual fulfillment is not found elsewhere, but here. This is the lesson of stability: if you cannot find God here, you will not be able to find him anywhere. Along with the monk's commitment to a geographical place is his commitment to a particular community of people. Benedict insists that wherever we are, we have others to love, and there is no point seeking some other community that might be easier to love or who might love us more. The difficult lessons of love are there to be learned right where we are.

If God is to be found in this particular place, then the vow of stability teaches that he is also to be found in this present moment. When confronted by the idea of her death, Thérèse says, "I do not trouble myself — I prefer to think only of the present moment."[29] "We must see life in its true light . . . it is an instant between two eternities!"[30] "Let us turn our single moment of suffering to profit, let us see each instant as if there were no other. An instant is a treasure."[31] The present moment is the opportunity to live in eternity now. The past is a vague memory and the future an uncertain fantasy. Reality is now and only now. Thérèse lives this momentary existence with a stunning vitality. So from the heart of her final suffering she says, "We who run in the way of Love must never torment ourselves about anything. If I did not suffer minute by minute, it would be impossible for me to be patient; but I see only the present moment, I forget the past, and take good care not to anticipate the future. If we grow disheartened, if sometimes we despair, it is because we have been dwelling on the past or the future."[32] "As far as she is concerned, a thing is not true unless it can be perfected in the moment-to-moment fulfilment of God's will."[33]

Benedict also stresses the need to redeem time by taking advantage of the present moment. With a sense of urgency Benedict rouses his sons in the Prologue: "Now is the hour for us to rise from sleep (Rom. 13.11). Let us, then, open our eyes to the divine light and hear with our ears the divine voice as it cries out to us daily. 'Today if you hear his voice do not harden your hearts' (Ps. 94.8)."[34]

Time cannot be wasted; "if we wish to escape the punishment of hell and reach eternal life then while there is still time, while we are still living in this body and this life gives us the light to do all these things, we must hurry now to do what will profit us for ever."[35]

It is at this point that Benedict's Rule of stability connects most intimately and dynamically with Thérèse's little way. The cornerstone of Thérèse's little way is that we find sanctity hidden in ordinary life — right here and right now. The same truth is hidden in Jesus' parables of the lost coin, the lost treasure in the field, the prodigal son, and the pearl of great price. In each case the treasure is a little thing hidden in the dust of a house, in a newly plowed field, in a pigpen, and in a merchant's stall. The hidden treasure is the truth that salvation is hidden in this present moment, and stability is the discipline that focuses our attention on the grimly joyful news that salvation is buried in the mud beneath our feet.

Finding eternal reality here and now is the burning heart of incarnation. The saint is able to see that each moment is electric with eternity. Benedict's attention to daily detail makes the point in a pure way. For St. Benedict the physical opportunities of every moment are a sacrament of spiritual realities. What happens in the kitchen is just as important as what happens in the church. Some of Benedict's most moving and meaningful chapters discuss how the brothers should serve one another in the most mundane ways. As they serve in the infirmary they are seen to be serving Christ in their sick brother.[36] Kitchen duty is not a dull chore, but an opportunity for divine service, and is therefore demanded of everyone.[37]

> The one who is finishing his week's duty does the
> washing on the Saturday; he should also wash the towels

with which the brethren dry their hands and feet. Moreover, he who is ending this week's service together with him who is about to start should wash the feet of all . . . the incoming and outgoing servers should prostrate themselves . . . at the feet of all the brethren in the oratory and ask to be prayed for. The outgoing server is to say the verse, 'Blessed are you, Lord God, for you have helped and strengthened me.' When this has been said three times, and he has received a blessing, the incoming server follows and says, 'O God, come to my aid; Lord, make haste to help me.'[38]

Benedict imbues ordinary tasks with spiritual meaning. His ritual for kitchen service echoes the foot washing of the Last Supper, and the communal meal in the refectory becomes an extension of the communion meal in the church. The versicles and responses in the kitchen also echo the antiphonal praises from the choir. Thus each small action becomes an act of faith, and in each moment of time eternity is unlocked.

Stability enables Thérèse to see the spiritual dimension radiating through her ordinary life as well. Balthasar observes, "Everything Thérèse achieves at the supernatural level is rooted in something she has experienced at the natural level."[39] The profound love and simple faith she experienced in her natural family immediately transferred to, and illuminated, her relationship — first to God, then to the monastery, then to the Church, and finally to the whole cosmos. As she was the little daughter and little sister in the Martin household she eventually became God's little daughter, Jesus' little sister, and the little sister of every Christian. For Thérèse the whole natural world was "charged with the grandeur of God." As Benedict saw Christ in the sick, Thérèse also wants to be in charge of the infirmary, saying, "Oh! How I wish I had been infirmarian . . . yes, I would have had an inclination for all that. And I'd have put so much love into the work, thinking of God's words: 'I was sick and you visited me.' "⁴⁰

As Benedict sees spiritual significance surging through service in the refectory, so Thérèse sees spiritual meaning in something as small as eating the food set before her. In the refectory she imagined in a childish way that she was sharing her food with the Holy Family.⁴¹ In another instance she could serve God in her sisters simply by tidying their clothes for them: "I applied myself above all to practice quite hidden little acts of virtue; thus I liked to fold the mantles forgotten by the Sisters."⁴²

This little way of daily service is possible for every soul. If heaven is hidden in little lives, then little people can find it. The stability of family life is enough for anyone to find inner stability. The commitment of marriage is a lifetime vow that requires stability to flourish. The self-sacrifice of looking after one's spouse and children is a satisfactory stairway to heaven. If Thérèse could find divine service in folding head scarves, and Benedict in washing table napkins, then we can find it in folding the laundry and setting the table.

The vow of stability means we must come face to face with the opportunities of this particular place, this particular time, and this particular set of people we live with. Stability therefore means we must face reality, the reality of ourselves, our loved ones, our decisions, our weakness, our confusion and fear. We must face our problems and realize that no one else is going to solve them for us. Often the truth hurts and reality appears grim, but we cannot have only the "nice" reality we create, for that is by definition unreality. The psychologist Scott Peck points out that we cannot have the good reality without the bad. If we try to avoid the bad sort of reality, we automatically miss the good as well. Thomas Merton says:

> The more you try to avoid suffering, the more you
> suffer, because smaller and more insignificant things be-
> gin to torture you ... the one who does most to avoid
> suffering is, in the end, the one who suffers most: and his
> suffering comes to him from things so little and so trivial
> that one can say that it is no longer objective at all; it is his
> own existence which is the source of his pain.[43]

If the vow of stability forces me to stay in one place and face the grim realities of my life, then I am also confronted by the glorious realities. Indeed, if we embrace the grim reality, then the good reality is more vibrantly alive than we could ever have imagined. The climax of Thérèse's deathbed experience was an excruciating participation in the suffering of Christ, but it was also an exhilarating participation in the love of Christ. On the afternoon of her death she cries, "Never would I have believed it was possible to suffer so much!"[44] but her last words are, "Oh! I love Him! . . . My God . . . I love you!"[45]

Immersion in ordinary reality demands a deep immersion in the life of all things. By the power of the incarnation, heaven is not "up there" and earth "down here." Instead heaven is there, born in a stable at a particular point in time; and if there and then, then also here and now. The kingdom of God is within not just my heart, but within all things; heaven surges in and through each person, each tree, and each blade of grass. Reality surges within joy and sorrow, death and life, loss and the gain, and it is the vow of stability that engages us with this concrete reality and cuts off our desire to run after an illusion.

Stability seems dull, but hidden in the heart of dull stability glows a mystic vision: a vision of radiant and universal Reality surging through all things. It is the vision of Dostoyevsky's

Alyosha. From the grim reality of his friend Zossima's coffin he wanders outside into the monastery garden.

> The vault of heaven, full of soft shining stars, stretched vast and fathomless above him. . . . The gorgeous autumn flowers, in the beds around the house were slumbering till morning. The silence of earth seemed to melt into the silence of the heavens. The mystery of earth was one with the mystery of the stars. Alyosha stood, gazed, and suddenly threw himself down on the earth. He did not know why he embraced it. He could not have told why he longed so irresistibly to kiss it, to kiss it all. But he kissed it weeping, sobbing and watering it with his tears and vowed passionately to love it, to love it forever and ever. . . . But with every instant he felt clearly, as it were tangibly, that something firm and unshakeable as that vault of heaven had entered into his soul.[46]

From that moment Alyosha leaves the monastery to go and sojourn in the world because at last he has begun to understand the world. It is a commitment to stability that grants an experience of mystic unity, for it is stability that forces us to look at the reality that surrounds us and so perceive the deeper reality that permeates it all.

Chapter Five Endnotes

1. Abbot Parry (tr.), *The Rule of St. Benedict*, Leominster, Gracewing, 1997, p. 94.
2. Ibid.
3. Ibid., pp. 7-8.
4. Ibid., p. 7.

5. Thomas Merton, *The Wisdom of the Desert*, London, Sheldon Press, 1960, p. 30.

6. John Clarke, O.C.D. (tr.), *The Story of a Soul: The Autobiography of St. Thérèse of Lisieux*, Washington, D.C., ICS Publications, 1976, p. 148.

7. F. J. Sheed (tr.), *Collected Letters of Saint Thérèse of Lisieux*, London, Sheed and Ward, 1949, p. 121.

8. John Clarke, O.C.D. (tr.), *General Correspondence, Vol. II*, Washington, D.C., ICS Publications, 1988, p. 831.

9. Parry, p. 95.

10. Ibid., p. 60.

11. Ibid.

12. Ibid., p. 58.

13. Ibid., p. 59.

14. Clarke, *The Story of a Soul*, p. 226.

15. John Clarke, O.C.D. (tr.), *St. Thérèse of Lisieux: Her Last Conversations*, Washington, D.C., ICS Publications, 1977, p. 197.

16. Ibid.

17. Letter to Mother Agnes.

18. Ibid.

19. 2 Corinthians 4:18.

20. Parry, p. 57.

21. Thomas Traherne, *Centuries of Meditations*, London, Faith Press, 1964, I.12.

22. Thomas Merton, *Conjectures of a Guilty Bystander*, New York, Doubleday, 1966, p. 140.

23. Henri J. M. Nouwen, *The Genesee Diary: Report from a Trappist Monastery*, New York, Doubleday, 1976, pp. 48-49.

24. Parry, p. 3.

25. Clarke, *The Story of a Soul*, p. 233.

26. Parry, p. 20.

27. Clarke, *[St. Thérèse's] Last Conversations*, p. 88.

28. Parry, p. 20.

29. I. F. Görres, *The Hidden Face: A Study of St. Thérèse of Lisieux*, New York, Pantheon, 1959, p. 377.

30. Clarke, *General Correspondence, Vol. I*, p. 553.

31. Ibid., p. 558.

32. An Irish Carmelite (tr.), *Thoughts of Saint Therese*, Rockford, Illinois, Tan Books, 1915, p. 97.

33. Hans Urs Von Balthasar, *Two Sisters in the Spirit*, San Francisco, Ignatius Press, 1970, p. 71.

34. Parry, p. 1.

35. Ibid., p. 4.

36. Ibid., p. 64.

37. Ibid., p. 62.

38. Ibid., pp. 62-63.

39. Balthasar, p. 125.

40. Clarke, *[St. Thérèse's] Last Conversations*, p. 156.

41. Ibid., p. 108.

42. Clarke, *The Story of a Soul*, p. 159.

43. Thomas Merton, *The Seven Storey Mountain*, London, SPCK, 1961, p. 82.

44. Clarke, *[St. Thérèse's] Last Conversations*, p. 205.

45. Ibid., p. 206.

46. Fyodor Dostoyevsky, *The Brothers Karamazov*, New York, Random House, 1950, p. 436.

Six

Childhood and Conversion of Life

Thoughts and Prayers

Jesus answered him, "Truly, truly, I say to you, unless one is born anew, he cannot see the kingdom of God."

— JOHN 3:3

For thus said the Lord GOD, the Holy One of Israel, / "In returning and rest you shall be saved; / in quietness and in trust shall be your strength."

— ISAIAH 30:15

Grace does not abolish nature, but perfects it.

— ST. THOMAS AQUINAS

The spiritual life is a long strange business and you've got to be quiet and docile enough to go on learning.

— IRIS MURDOCH

Life is only for Love;
Time is only to find God.

— ST. BERNARD

Prayer
Lord, make me according to your heart.

— BROTHER LAWRENCE

Abbot Lot, one of the Desert Fathers, came to Abbot Joseph and said, "Father, according as I am able, I keep my little rule, and my little fast, my prayer, meditation and contemplative silence; and according as I am able I strive to cleanse my heart of thoughts: now what more should I do?" The elder rose up in reply and stretched out his hands to heaven, and his fingers became like ten lamps of fire. He said, "Why not be totally changed into fire?"[1]

A person may have a conversion experience in a variety of ways ranging from the backwoods religion of the revivalist preacher to the sublime beauty of an English cathedral; but while conversion experiences happen within religion, they do not require religion. Through a breathtaking experience of beauty, love, or grief, a soul can transcend the mundane and be "converted," if only for a moment. In an unexpected instant one can glimpse the "intersection of the timeless moment,"[2] when the whisper of eternity is half-heard in the stillness. No matter how enlightening it is, a conversion experience is not the same thing as conversion of life. A person may have an experience that transforms one's way of seeing, but "conversion of life" transforms that person's way of being. Conversion experiences are powerful emotional events, but if there is nothing more than emotion, then the conversion experience is more experience than conversion, and the result is not spiritual rebirth but a spiritual stillbirth.

Conversion may begin in transcendence, but it must end with transformation. Conversion of life is just what it says it is: the conversion of one's whole existence. Beyond any doubt the Pharisee called Saul was changed when Christ knocked him off his high horse on the road to Damascus; but St. Paul had to forge that moment of conversion into a lifetime of conversion. Years later he was still saying, "Not that I . . . am already perfect; but I press on to make it my own, because Christ Jesus has already made me his own. . . . I press on toward the goal for the prize of the upward call of God in Christ Jesus. Let those of us who are mature be thus minded."[3]

When something is converted, it is changed from one thing to another; and when a person is converted, he is changed from being one kind of person to another. That's why, throughout the Scriptures, when a person is converted, he gets a new name that signifies that he is a new creation. At the heart of conversion is the little word *metanoia*, which is used for repentance but which means "change." *Metanoia* means a profound change of mind, heart, and viewpoint. For conversion of life to be real we must maintain a *metanoia* mentality; in other words we must have a mindset that is always expecting transformation.

Because conversion means finding a new way of seeing, even little children — especially little children — can experience the grace of conversion. Part of having a *metanoia* mentality is to be always open and learning. Children are natural learners; they are inquisitive and believing. They are able to follow their spiritual instincts without the accumulated burdens of cynicism, doubt, or fear. In this natural way Benedict and Thérèse were converted as children. Gregory the Great describes Benedict's boyhood, which evidenced a *metanoia* mentality from the start. By instinct he turned away from worldly amusements and was naturally detached from selfish pleasures.

> During his boyhood he showed mature understanding, and a strength of character far beyond his years kept his heart detached from every pleasure. Even while still living in the world, free to enjoy all it had to offer he saw how empty it was and turned from it without regret.[4]

Remembering her childhood, Thérèse expresses the same disappointment with "the world." "God gave me the grace of knowing the *world* just enough to despise it and separate myself from it."[5]

This turning away from "the world" is not a personality disorder, puritanism, or pessimism. While Thérèse turns away from worldliness she does not turn away from the world. Instead the child Thérèse is enraptured by the natural world and sees God everywhere. She reads eternal messages in a storm or a starry night, in a poor cripple, a school prize giving, or a visit to the sea:

> I was six or seven years old when Papa brought us to Trouville. Never will I forget the impression the sea made upon me; I couldn't take my eyes off it since its majesty, the roaring of its waves, everything spoke to my soul of God's grandeur and power. . . . In the evening at that moment when the sun seems to bathe itself in the immensity of the wave, leaving a luminous trail behind, I went and sat down on the huge rock with Pauline. . . . I contemplated this luminous trail for a long time. It was to me the image of God's grace shedding its light across the path the little white-sailed vessel had to travel and . . . I made the resolution never to wander far away from the glance of Jesus in order to travel peacefully toward the eternal shore.[6]

In the child the mature person is present in seed form, and the conversions that happen in childhood are usually the most profound, even if they take place at an immature age. Such conversions are profound because there is not much for God to overcome in an inexperienced child. A child who opens his heart to

God does so with an innocent trust that the adult can never regain, and so God's grace in the young life is especially strong. Benedict and Thérèse looked to greater things when they were children, and those miniature visions of faith grew into a more radical conversion in their adolescence.

As a youth Benedict was sent from his patrician home to study in Rome, but he soon realized it wasn't for him. Gregory says:

> When he found many of the students there abandoning themselves to vice, he decided to withdraw from the world he had been preparing to enter; for he was afraid that if he acquired any of its learning he would be drawn down with them. In his desire to please God alone, he turned his back on further studies, gave up home and inheritance and resolved to embrace the religious life.[7]

Thérèse experienced the same change of mind that went with a change of location. "At the age of ten the heart allows itself to be easily dazzled," she writes, "and I consider it a great grace not to have remained at Alençon. The friends we had there were too worldly."[8]

Like Benedict, Thérèse continued her life's conversion in adolescence. She describes a conversion experience that happened when she was thirteen. "It was on December the twenty-fifth, 1886, that I was given the grace to leave my childhood days behind; call it, if you will, the grace of complete conversion."[9] Thérèse describes how she was disappointed by her father's impatient comment about her and the fuss over Christmas presents. For years she had suffered from hypersensitivity and a guilty conscience. Suddenly the cloud lifted and she felt an outpouring of grace. Her life was transformed. Her vision widened. Her childish selfishness vanished. She calls it "a sublime reality."[10] As Thérèse wrote of her conversion on Christmas Day 1886, "to put it quite simply, charity had found its way into my heart, calling on me to forget myself and try to bring happiness to others; and since then I've been as happy as the day is long."[11]

Benedict enshrines "conversion of life" as one of the three vows for his monks. "The one who is to be accepted into the community must promise in the oratory, in the presence of all, stability, conversion of life and obedience."[12] The fact that Benedict makes conversion of life one of the vows drives home the fact that while conversion of life cannot be achieved without God's grace, it also cannot be achieved without human determination. Conversion of life requires total commitment, so Benedict rallies his sons, saying: "We must make ready our hearts and bodies to engage in the warfare of holy obedience to his commands, and because our nature has not power to do this, we must ask God to send forth the help of his grace to our aid . . . we must hurry to do now what will profit us for ever."[13]

The vow of conversion of life is the most dynamic and demanding of the three Benedictine vows because it calls for constant change. Cardinal Newman observed that change is one of the sure signs of life, so the one who seeks conversion of life is seeking to change his life constantly. This constant push for change balances the vow of stability and keeps stability from becoming stagnant. In stability we put down roots; in conversion of life we spread our branches in growth. Stability is always content, but conversion of life is curious. Conversion of life is the water flowing over the waterfall. Stability is the cliff beneath.

Conversion of life also balances obedience. In obedience we submit, almost unquestioningly, to the higher authorities. The call to conversion of life, however, is a call to challenge ourselves and others. Conversion of life keeps obedience from turning us into mute slaves. The vow to convert our lives gives direction and struggle to our obedience. If our lives are to be converted, then every scrap and detail must be changed. Conversion of life is never complacent — it is the rebel of the vows, it has questions and demands answers. Obedience may submit, but conversion of life questions the command — seeking to understand the reason and the goal of obedience. Obedience lies prostrate on the floor. Conversion of life finds an ant crawling across the pavement, wonders at it, and learns a lesson from the ant. Obedience and stability are thus subject to a higher calling — they are both directed toward the higher goal of conversion of life.

Stability is secure. Obedience is hard and certain; but conversion of life is open-ended. As Esther deWaal has written:

> It means we have to live provisionally, ready to respond to the new whenever and however that might appear. There is no security here, no clinging to past certainties. Rather we must expect to see our chosen idols successively broken. It means a constant letting go. It is . . . the living out in daily life of the biblical demands . . . 'forgetting what is behind me, and reaching out for that which lies ahead, I press towards the goal to win the prize which is God's call to the life above, in Christ Jesus. (Phil. 3.13)[14]

Benedict's three vows work together as a little icon of the Holy Trinity. As the three persons of the Godhead are a unity, so the three vows work together in a dynamic unity. Stability is like God the Father — the rock upon which we build, the unchanging Ancient of Days. Obedience is reflected in the role of God the Son. Jesus Christ was the one who said to the Father, "Not my will, but yours be done." He was the one who was "obedient unto death." In his obedience Jesus Christ proves his unity with the Father; so as we seek to obey God, we connect on a profound level with the rich permanence and eternity of the Godhead. If stability points to God the Father and obedience points to God the Son, then conversion of life points to the creative force of the Holy Spirit. Conversion of life is the driving force, the expression and outworking of stability and obedience in our lives. Conversion of life becomes the force of unity and love that binds us to the other two vows of obedience and stability, and all three take us into the heart of the mystery of the triune God.

When Genesis says we are created in the image of God, it also means we are created in his triune image. Each person is a miniature Trinity. Various theologians have divided the human personality into two, three, or four parts. Some see body and soul. Some see body, mind, and spirit, while others see body, mind, spirit, and soul. Seeing the human person as threefold reflects back the truth that we are made in our Creator's image. If we are body, mind, and spirit, then we too reflect the Trinity. The mind reflects God the Father; the physical body reflects the Son who took on human flesh; our spirit or soul reflects the Holy Spirit — the eternal creative force between mind and body. These three parts of our person are refreshed and nurtured by the threefold Benedictine vows. Stability helps our mind to be renewed. The stable person is not double-minded. His mind is fixed on God alone. As Benedict says, he "prefers nothing above the love of Christ." Our bodies are most often the part of us that simply needs to obey. As the physical side of the Godhead, Jesus Christ, was the obedient one, so the physical side of our natures is disciplined and channeled by the Benedictine vow of obedience. Conversion of life connects with our Spirit — the eternal, dynamic part of us. This is the essence of our being, and it is the conversion of our soul-spirit that is the objective of our whole existence. Because we are a little Trinity, and because the vows are a little Trinity, the vows function together to bring us into a new unity of being.

While the three vows work together to change our life, Benedict never understands them as an end in themselves. The Rule is clear that the vows and rules of the religious life are not there to be fulfilled like some dull set of rubrics. Instead the whole monastic way, and every rule of life, is established in order to create the environment for holiness to grow. Benedict likens the monastery to a workshop or a school; it is not the end, but the means to the end.

The end of the journey is total conversion of life. We are not converted into something strange and new, but into something old and familiar. Plato said learning was simply remembering something we have forgotten, and conversion of life is being restored to a childlike condition that was lost long ago. It is hearing distant music and recognizing a long-forgotten melody. It is relearning how to be free. This conversion is not so much a transformation as a restoration. It is taking us back to the Garden, to reclaim a state of innocence lost.

Conversion of life means becoming as little children. This Gospel doctrine is foreshadowed in the Old Testament when the grown-up Syrian general goes to see the prophet Elisha. Naaman was infected with leprosy, and a little Israelite servant girl told him the prophet could heal him. Naaman did all the usual grown-up things. He went to see the king with gifts; he arrived at the prophet's house with his impressive retinue. When Naaman finally obeyed the prophet and dipped himself in the Jordan River, the Scripture says his leprous flesh looked like a little child's. For Naaman to be converted he had to become as a little child. If you like, he had to become as little as the servant girl who witnessed to him.

Conversion may mean becoming as little children, but it also means becoming properly mature. God began the conversion of Benedict's and Thérèse's lives in their childhood, and paradoxically, while their adulthood was innocent, their childhood was mature. Gregory says of Benedict, "During his boyhood he showed mature understanding, and a strength of character far beyond his years."[15] At school Thérèse was put in a class with children several years older than her, and she still finished at the top of the class. She often found playtime with other children difficult, explaining that "I didn't know how to play like other children and as a consequence wasn't a very pleasant companion. I did my best, however, to imitate them, but without much success. I was very much bored by it all."[16]

She was bored, not because she was a snob, but because she was already mature beyond her years.

The converted soul brings innocence to adulthood— and maturity to childhood. Thérèse expounds this paradox in her discussion of her Christmas conversion experience of 1886. Although her conversion experience was a "grace to leave her childhood days behind," she says elsewhere that her conversion was the discovery of her "childhood character."[17] Both are true; in the converted life every fault of grown-up life must be transformed into a childlike virtue, and every childish fault must be outgrown. Whatever the person's chronological age, grown-up cynicism must be changed to faith, despair to hope, and hatred to love; but likewise childish greed and selfishness must be converted into generosity, patience, and loving kindness. Thus the converted soul holds the wisdom of age in a playful tension with the innocence and trust of childhood.

When this conversion process is consolidated, we are restored not to some superhuman state, but to a supra-human state.

We are not less human, but more human. We are free to do all that we should do because it has become natural. This is why the saints are the true humanists, because they reveal the pinnacle of human potential. In the saints we meet individuals who have been so totally converted that they have become who they really are. In contrast, the rest of us are less than ourselves. Without total conversion we are scraps of potential converts huddling behind the various masks we present to the world. Without conversion we are mere hints and shadows of all we might be. If we could only glimpse our glorious true potential, we would fall back in amazement and shame that there is still so much work to be done and that we have wasted so much time.

Benedict makes it clear that the converted life is one that is driven and fueled by the fire of love. When Abbot Joseph said the aim was to be changed into a burning lamp of fire, he meant that the Holy Spirit should so fill our lives that we are burning with love for God and love for other people in our whole lives. For Benedict conversion of life means not simply learning how to love, but being consumed and transformed into love. In the final words of the Rule he sums up this life of love:

> No one should pursue what he thinks advantageous for himself, but rather what seems best for another. They should labor with chaste love at the charity of the brotherhood. They should fear God. They should love their Abbot with sincere and humble charity. They should prefer nothing whatever to Christ.[18]

Thérèse also realizes that total conversion of life means being consumed by Love. If she knew it, she would sing with gusto the hymn, "Come down, O Love Divine, fill thou this soul of mine and visit it with Thine own ardour glowing." Her awareness that Love was the key to conversion came suddenly, like a little conversion itself as she read 1 Corinthians 13. In one of her most exalted and intimate passages she writes:

> I continued my readings and this sentence consoled me: 'yet strive after the better gifts, and I point out to you a yet more excellent way.' And the Apostle explains how all the most perfect gifts are nothing without love. That Charity is the excellent way that leads most surely to God. I finally had rest. . . . Charity gave me the key to my vocation. I understood that if the Church had a body composed of different members, the most necessary and most noble of all could not be lacking to it, and so I understood that the Church had a heart and that this heart was burning with love. Then in the excess of my delirious joy I cried out, 'O Jesus, my Love . . . my vocation, at last I have found it . . . my vocation is love! . . . Why speak of a delirious joy? No, this expression is not exact, for it was rather the calm and serene peace of the navigator perceiving the beacon which must lead him to the port. . . . O luminous Beacon of love, I know how to reach you, I have found the secret of possessing your flame.'[19]

Balthasar observes: "Just as a watch or a machine with dancing dolls or a music box will stop if the spring is broken, so the whole action of the Church would come to a standstill if the contemplative love at the heart of it all were to cease. And so love increases in the life of each and every vocation, because it is essentially universal."[20]

Thérèse cries:

> I realised that this love was the true motive force which
> enabled the other members of the Church to act; if it ceased
> to function the Apostles would forget to preach the gos-
> pel, the Martyrs would refuse to shed their blood. Love, in
> fact, is the vocation which includes all the others; it's a
> universe of its own, comprising all time and space — it's
> eternal . . . I had discovered where it is that I belong in the
> Church, the place God has appointed for me. To be noth-
> ing else than love, deep down in the heart of Mother
> Church; that's to be everything at once.[21]

Thérèse takes Benedict's conversion of life to the final point.
For Thérèse conversion of life does not simply mean becoming
more loving — it means her life is converted into Love itself. In
this conversion the ego is not obliterated but transcended. Being converted into Love means the soul becomes united with
God's love. Echoing the Abbot Joseph, who said, "Why not be
totally transformed into fire?" Thérèse writes:

> What is it then to ask to be 'drawn' if not to be united
> in an intimate way to the object which captivates our heart?
> If fire and iron had the use of reason, and if the latter said
> to the other: 'Draw me,' would it not prove that it desires
> to be identified with the fire in such a way that the fire
> penetrates and drinks it up with its burning substance and
> seems to become one with it? This is my prayer: I ask Jesus
> to draw me into the flames of his love, to unite me so closely
> to Him that He lives and acts in me.[22]

The nature of love is that it lays down its life, and therefore
the more we love the more we sacrifice ourselves for others, and

the more we sacrifice ourselves the more we are consumed by love. Thérèse's language of Love is sublime, but where her doctrine is most sublime, it is also most terrible. For her to become a living flame and share in Christ's redemption she must be transformed, and that means her earthly life will be consumed. It is a terrible irony that the very illness that destroyed her is called consumption. At this point the only language that makes sense of the mystery is the language of sacrifice. It is not a pious sentimentality that makes Thérèse see herself as a martyr and a sacrificial lamb. She wants to be immolated on the altar of love and nothing less than that will suffice. Only this desire to be a sacrifice of Love can explain the terrible words of a girl in her twenties.

> I cannot confine myself to desiring one kind of martyrdom. To satisfy me I need *all*. Like You, my Adorable Spouse, I would be scourged and crucified. I would die flayed like St. Bartholomew, I would be plunged into boiling oil like St. John; I would undergo all the tortures inflicted upon the martyrs. With St. Agnes and St. Cecilia, I would present my neck to the sword and like Joan of Arc, my dear sister, I would whisper at the stake Your Name, O JESUS.[23]

Thérèse realizes that for her life to be totally converted, for her to be transformed into a cosmic fire of love, she must be one of Christ's co-sufferers, thus her intimate devotion to the Holy Face. Thérèse wants her face to be seen in Christ's face, and his suffering face to be reflected in hers. Like St. Paul she wants to be "crucified with Christ."[24] So Thérèse writes:

> In order to live in one single act of perfect Love, I offer myself as a victim of holocaust to Your merciful Love,

asking You to consume me incessantly, allowing the waves of infinite tenderness shut up within You to overflow into my soul, and that thus I may become a martyr of Your Love, O my God![25]

"It is precisely through becoming zero, through accepting her complete unimportance, that the miraculous, total fulfilment of grace is accomplished."[26] Thérèse writes, "I am nothing but a weak and helpless child, but it is my very weakness that gives me the courage to offer myself as a victim of your love, O Jesus . . . in order to be completely satisfied love must stoop even to nothingness and transform this nothingness into fuel for its flame."[27]

Thérèse's insistence on being a spiritual child is the very point at which she presumes to make such a universal offering of love. "I should fear to be overwhelmed beneath the weight of my bold desires! My excuse is that I am a child; and children do not reflect on the meaning of their words."[28]

Most importantly, if this conversion process is the transformation of one's life into a consuming Love, then it also means we are being transformed into the likeness of Christ Jesus. Thérèse recounts her fusion with the Love, which is Christ, at her first communion:

I felt that I was loved. There were no demands made, no struggles, no sacrifices; for a long time now Jesus and poor little Thérèse looked at and understood each other. That day, it was no longer simply a look, it was a fusion; they were no longer two, Thérèse had vanished as a drop of water is lost in the immensity of the ocean. Jesus alone remained.[29]

In her *Act of Oblation to Merciful Love* she wrote, "I cannot receive Holy Communion as often as I desire, but Lord, are You not all-powerful? Remain in me as in a tabernacle and never separate Yourself from Your little victim."[30] "Mother Agnes of Jesus, Thérèse's sister Pauline, was asked by the tribunal set up in 1911 to investigate the life and virtues of Thérèse, whether this request that Jesus remain in her as in a tabernacle was meant by Thérèse in a metaphorical sense or was to be taken literally. Mother Agnes's reply was that she was certain that the words were meant literally."[31]

St. Paul also longs for this mystic union with the suffering Christ when he says, "I want to know Christ and the power of his resurrection and the fellowship of sharing in his sufferings becoming like him in his death, and so somehow to attain to the resurrection of the dead."[32] So he gets to the point where he can say, "I have been crucified with Christ; it is no longer I who live, but Christ who lives in me."[33]

When Thérèse says this suffering is her role in the Church, she expresses a profound theological truth. Through our baptism we are members of that same Body because through baptism we are all "baptized into the death of Christ." The child who is baptized is the same sacrificial lamb that Thérèse reveals. At our baptism we were offered, and the essence of that offering is the dynamic force of baptism alive in each Christian's life. Even if it lies dormant, the grace of baptism is a child's offering, a promise to follow Christ in the path of sacrificial love. Thérèse fulfills her baptism as few have ever done before her, and her embrace of sacrificial love is the cross all of us must take up if we too are to have our lives converted into the Christ-life completely. As St. Paul teaches, "Therefore be imitators of God, as beloved children. And walk in love, as Christ loved us and gave himself up for us, a fragrant offering and sacrifice to God."[34]

The three vows that lead to this self-sacrifice are intimately bound up with the Holy Trinity, and it was on the Feast of the

Holy Trinity in 1895 that Thérèse offered herself in her *Act of Oblation to Merciful Love*. In a most fervent prayer she wrote, "I wish to fulfil Your will perfectly and attain the degree of glory You have prepared for me in Your kingdom. In a word, I desire to be a saint."[35]

Thérèse's desire for sacrifice seems sick to some and absurd to others, but even for those who begin to understand the mystery of her sacrifice the idea of such total offering of oneself is a terrifying act of surrender. Such heroism seems beyond the reach of most Christians. Every important statement has a key phrase, and the key in Thérèse's heroic prayer are the words "the degree of glory You have prepared for me." While all Christ's disciples are called to conversion and called to carry a cross, God does not call all his children to the same degree of glory or the same form of sacrifice. Benedict instructs the abbot to take special care of each of the souls in his charge because God works in each individual in a unique way. He explains: "The Abbot . . . must realise how difficult and arduous is the task he has undertaken, that of ruling souls and serving men of many different characters; one to be encouraged, another to be rebuked, another persuaded, each according to his nature and intelligence. Thus he must adapt and fit himself to all."[36]

To illustrate God's unique work in each individual Thérèse recalls an incident from her childhood:

> Pauline told me to fetch Papa's large tumbler and set it alongside my thimble and filled both to the brim with water. She asked me which one was fuller. I told her each was as full as the other and that it was impossible to put more water than they could contain. . . . God in heaven will grant His elect as much glory as they can take, the last having nothing to envy in the first.[37]

The question is not whether we have done great things for God, but whether we have allowed him to do great things for us. "I understood too that our Lord's love is revealed as perfectly in the most simple soul who resists His grace in nothing as in the most excellent soul."[38]
Von Balthasar explains:

> The fulfilment of God's will does not mean carrying out an anonymous universal law that is the same for all; nor does it mean the slavish imitation of some fixed blueprint — like a child reproducing a pattern on tracing paper. . . . God reckons with the unique nature, strength and capacity of each individual. Nevertheless, he deals with us freely. . . . It is not possible, by simply assessing a person's nature, to predict God's gracious intentions for him, the idea of sanctity to which he must conform or the sacrifices it will require of him, though we can predict quite certainly that sacrifices will be demanded of him, since all love involves self-denial. Each one of us has to experience and grow attentive to God's sanctifying will in prayer and meditation; outside prayer there is no means of discerning our path to sanctity.[39]

Balthasar recognizes two basic types of holiness: "On the one hand 'customary' sanctity, by which the Christian fulfils his vocation through the normal, unspectacular round of the Church's life; on the other hand, a special type of sanctity, by which God singles out some individual for the good of the Church and the community as a model of sanctity."[40]
The first type of heroic saint has a mission that "flashes across the dome of the Church like lightning from heaven and lights up unmistakably some unique point of God's will for

the Church."[41] These souls, like Thérèse and Benedict, are given a special mission from God, and special strength to complete that mission. Even though they are not possible to imitate, these are the saints who become the favorites of the faithful. They are so, not because they can be imitated, but because they reveal "a new type of conformity to Christ inspired by the Holy Spirit and therefore a new illustration of how the Gospel is to be lived."[42]

Benedict and Thérèse are heroic in this way. Both saints seem impossible to imitate, but both offer a fresh way of living the Gospel. When Thérèse offers the little way of spiritual childhood and Benedict offers a "little Rule for beginners," they give a fresh teaching about living the sacrifice of the Gospel through ordinary life. Their teaching is driven by their lives, and while we look to their lives for inspiration it is to their teaching that we look for possibilities. Thérèse and Benedict's teachings are complementary. Benedict offers mature stability and the wisdom of age. Thérèse balances that with youthful idealism and fiery enthusiasm. In his stress on Christ's presence within the warp and woof of ordinary life Benedict teaches us that in the ordinary routine we may find sanctity waiting. In her fervent insistence on the little way without heroics Thérèse puts Benedict's tools of good works into our hands. With the encouragement of this little sister and father in the faith we can take up our own vow to pursue a total transformation of our life empowered by the grace of God.

Conversion of life means adopting spiritual childhood — a childhood in which maturity and youth dance together, like an old man and his granddaughter at a wedding. St. Paul sums up this total conversion in his words to the Church at Ephesus. Like Thérèse we are to be young and alive, and like Benedict we are to be mature and stable.

St. Paul says that we should "live as children of light . . . being made new in the attitude of our minds, we must put on the new self, created to be like God in true righteousness and holiness . . . until we all reach unity in the faith and in the knowledge of the Son of God and become mature, attaining to the whole measure of the fullness of Christ."[43]

Chapter Six Endnotes

1. Thomas Merton, *The Wisdom of the Desert,* London, Sheldon Press, 1960, p. 50.

2. T. S. Eliot, *The Four Quartets,* London, Faber and Faber, 1986, p. 42.

3. Philippians 3:12-15.

4. Odo Zimmerman, O.S.B., and Benedict Avery, O.S.B. (tr.), *Life and Miracles of St. Benedict* (Book II of the *Dialogues*), Prologue, Collegeville, Minnesota, The Liturgical Press, 1987.

5. John Clarke, O.C.D. (tr.); *The Story of a Soul: The Autobiography of St. Thérèse of Lisieux,* Washington, D.C., ICS Publications, 1976, p. 73.

6. Ibid., p. 48.

7. Zimmerman and Avery, *Life and Miracles of St. Benedict,* Prologue.

8. Clarke, *The Story of a Soul,* p. 73.

9. Ronald Knox (tr.), *Autobiography of a Saint,* London, Collins, 1973, p. 101.

10. Ibid., p. 102.

11. Ibid., p. 101.

12. Abbot Parry (tr.), *The Rule of St. Benedict,* Leominster, Gracewing, 1997, p. 94.

13. Ibid., p. 4.

14. Esther de Waal, *Seeking God,* London, Fount Paperbacks, 1988, p. 70.

15. Zimmerman and Avery, *Life and Miracles of St. Benedict,* Prologue.

16. Clarke, *The Story of a Soul,* p. 54.

17. Ibid., p. 34.

18. Parry, p.116.

19. Clarke, *The Story of a Soul,* pp.194-195.

20. Hans Urs Von Balthasar, *Two Sisters in the Spirit,* Ignatius Press, San Francisco, 1970, p. 203.

21. Knox, p. 146.

22. Clarke, *The Story of a Soul,* p. 257.

23. Ibid., p.193.

24. Cf. Galatians 2:20.

25. Clarke, *The Story of a Soul,* p. 277.

26. Balthasar, p. 204.

27. Knox, p. 186.

28. Clarke, *The Story of a Soul,* p. 196.

29. Ibid., p. 77.

30. Ibid., p. 276.

31. John Nelson, *Living the Little Way of Love,* London, New City, 1999, p. 166.

32. Philippians 3:10.

33. Galatians 2:20.

34. Ephesians 5:1-2.

35. Clarke, *The Story of a Soul,* p. 276.

36. Parry, p. 13.

37. Clarke, *The Story of a Soul,* p. 45.

38. Ibid., p. 14.

39. Balthasar, p. 21.

40. Ibid., p. 22.

41. Ibid., p. 23.

42. Ibid., p. 25.

43. Ephesians 5:8; 4:23; 4:13.

Seven

The Ascent of Humility

Thoughts and Prayers

Whoever humbles himself like this child, he is the greatest in the kingdom of heaven.

— Matthew 18:4

O Lord, my heart is not lifted up, / my eyes are not raised too high; / I do not occupy myself with things too great and too marvelous for me. / But I have calmed and quieted my soul, / like a child quieted at its mother's breast; / like a child that is quieted is my soul.

— Psalm 131:1-2

I'm a Nobody! Who are you?
Are you — nobody too?

— Emily Dickinson

'Tis a gift to be simple,
'Tis a gift to be free,
'Tis a gift to come down where we ought to be.
And when you've come down to the place that's right,
You'll be in the valley of love and delight.

— Shaker hymn

God always approaches man from beneath
and man must always stoop to meet Him.

— Nicholas Zernov

Prayer
Lord, never suffer us to think that we can stand by ourselves.

— John Donne

Humility is a dangerous virtue because it threatens to kill the person we love most: ourselves. Beneath the sweet face of humility is a mortal threat to our deformed ego; and because we hate what we fear, humility is not only dangerous but despised. Furthermore, we kill what we fear. As a result, the little child Humility is not only despised — she is destroyed. The twentieth century proves this to be true. In every continent as the man of power rose up, the humble children of faith were trampled into the mud. The blood of the modern martyrs cries out the truth that humility is always maimed and murdered.

One of the reasons humility is murdered is because it is misunderstood. Humility is often mistaken for obsequiousness, but obsequious people are rarely humble, while humble people are never obsequious. The root of the word "humility" is humus or soil, so humility means being down-to-earth. The person who is down-to-earth has got his feet on the ground. He has accepted all that is natural and good. Humble people are simple without being simpletons and servants without being servile. In fact, the humble person always bears an unmistakable air of dignity. The truly humble person is the most dignified person in the world, while those who stand on their dignity are the saddest sort of buffoons.

The person who stands on his dignity is standing on a very shaky ladder because one of the most popular jokes is to see a pompous person fall. Everyone laughs when the Lord Mayor's trousers fall down and feels a little pleased when the bishop who carries a crook turns out to *be* a crook. The word "humor" rightly shares the same root as "humility," and a humble person is one who always retains a sense of humor. This doesn't mean that the humble person is necessarily a comedian, but it does mean that such a person sees life as a comedy. Not every saint is a joker, but every saint realizes he is a joke. That is to say, the saints realize more than anyone that they are players in a cosmic drama, which seen from our perspective is a tragedy and seen from God's is a comedy. When Julian of Norwich says, "All shall be well and all manner of things shall be well," she is affirming the truth that, like every comedy, the final act will have a happy ending. As a result, the humble person is never permanently long-faced. Even in the midst of the most terrible suffering, the humble are in touch with that stupendous joy that rocks the universe.

Thérèse's superior said she was "a little innocent thing . . . whose head is filled with tricks to be played on anyone she pleases. . . . A mystic, a comedienne, she is everything! . . . She can make you shed tears of devotion and she can as easily make you split your sides with laughter."[1] In the midst of her introspective writings Thérèse always communicates an unmistakable *joie de vivre*. There is a lightness to her touch, and even on her terrible deathbed she shares puns and inside jokes with her sisters.

Gregory the Great is intent on showing us Benedict the wonder-working holy man, but in his biography of the saint, Gregory also reveals a matter-of-fact character who gets on with life, rather nonplussed by the fuss others make over his holiness. One can almost see his good-natured exasperation as he produces a necessary miracle here or a healing there. His down-to-earth approach is reminiscent of the story told of St. Thomas Aquinas who was taken to see a nun who was famous for levitating. When the saint saw her floating up to the ceiling, he remarked dryly, "I didn't know nuns had such big feet."

If humility is mistaken for servility and a dour demeanor, it is also mistaken for a poor self-image. The droopy person who thinks himself quite awful is guilty of a lack of love because he does not love himself. It is fashionable to "improve our self-image" with sad and shallow efforts like diets, cosmetic surgery, mind-control techniques, or self-help courses. One self-help guru advocates the constant repetition of the mantra "I like myself, I like myself, I like myself." Such self-brainwashing is as useless as it is ridiculous, and it is sadly distant from the virtue of humility. On the other hand, humility is also far from the mindset that repeats endlessly, "I hate myself, I hate myself, I hate myself." Both approaches evidence a twisted sort of pride. To like myself without discrimination is an error of judgment, and hating myself is a kind of self-deception. In contrast, humility is clear-sighted about the self. The humble person knows she has good traits and bad, but she works hard to control the bad while praising God for the good. Thérèse writes:

> It seems to me that if a little flower could speak, it would tell simply what God has done for it without trying to hide its blessings. It would not say, under the pretext of a false humility it is not beautiful or without perfume, that the sun has taken away its splendour and the storm has broken its stem when it knows that all this is untrue.[2]

Humility is down-to-earth, lighthearted, and realistic because it is the fruit of seeing ourselves from the eternal perspective. From God's point of view we are loved with an unconditional and everlasting love, so we are infinitely worthwhile. At the same time, we are only His creatures, and in the span of time and space we are a passing fleck of dust. Because of both truths we come to a state of "little-ness." We have found our place. We are hidden in the hollow of God's hand. Benedict recognizes the childlike quality of this trust in God and quotes Psalm 131: "Lord, my heart has no lofty ambitions, my eyes do not look too high; I am not concerned with great affairs or marvels beyond my scope. Why thus? 'If I did not think humbly, but exalted my soul, as a child on the mother's breast is weaned, so did you treat my soul.' "[3]

One of Thérèse's favorite verses from the Old Testament offers a similar image in support of the little way of spiritual childhood: "You shall be carried at the breasts, and upon the knees they shall caress you. As one whom the mother caresses so will I comfort you."[4] Because humility is about being little, it lies at the heart of Benedict's little Rule for beginners and the little way of Thérèse. Humility is inscribed on almost every page of Thérèse's story, and Benedict not only gives one of his major chapters to the virtue of humility, he also returns to the theme time and time again.

Like the monastic Fathers before him, Benedict believes that humility can be acquired. Humility is not essentially a lowly feeling about oneself, but the proper assessment of the self before God. This realistic attitude can be developed, and Benedict sets out a plan to do so. At the beginning of his chapter on humility, Benedict likens the spiritual quest to climbing Jacob's ladder.[5] The sides of the ladder are the body and soul and "in them the divine call inserts the diverse rungs of humility and interior discipline."[6] Benedict borrowed this idea from the earlier monastic writer John Cassian. Cassian warns that although the ladder has twelve rungs, it should not be understood as a step-by-step progress to perfection. Instead the twelve rungs of the ladder are twelve traits of the humble person. The twelve traits may develop progressively, but they will also exist together. Benedict points out the paradox of the ladder of humility: Going up means going down, and going down means going up. In other words, "going down and up is to be understood by us in the sense that we go down through pride and up through humility."[7] Commenting on Thérèse, Balthasar says, "Progress does not come through acquisitions but through losing everything; it does not mean climbing, it means descending."[8] Thérèse says to a novice, "You are wanting to climb a great mountain, and the good God is trying to make you descend it; he is waiting for you at the bottom in the fertile valley of humility."[9]

The twelve traits of humility that Father Benedict explains in his Rule, Sister Thérèse exemplifies in her life. Benedict writes quite a long treatise about the first rung of the ladder. "The first step of humility is for a man to set the fear of God always before his eyes and to utterly avoid forgetfulness."[10] It is a catchphrase that someone "puts the fear of God" in us. For Benedict it is no catchphrase. Being aware of God's presence means having fear of his judgment.

Benedict's monk "must always remember all God's commandments, and constantly turn over in his heart how hell will burn those who despise Him by their sins . . . at every moment a man must be on his guard against sins and vice — vices of thought, word, hand, foot or self-will, and also against the desires of the flesh. He must recognise that he is at every hour in the sight of God in heaven and that his actions are everywhere visible to the divine eyes of God."[11]

Such rollicking hellfire and brimstone preaching is rare today apart from the revivalist preachers in the murky backwoods of television. We're rather embarrassed to hear about a God who keeps the fires of hell stoked for the reception of sinners, but in polite society we are often embarrassed by what we fear. We shouldn't dismiss the fear of God just because we're frightened. When the Book of Proverbs says that "the fear of the Lord is the beginning of wisdom,"[12] it must be pointing to something more profound than medieval visions of a gloating God and grimacing demons with pitchforks. The fear of God and the fear of punishment are bound up with our complex relationship with God as Father. Since in infancy the father is the significant

Other, it is natural for us to fear him. We instinctively fear him because he is big and we are small; he is strong and we are weak. Our fear of the Father should mature into a love for the Father, but love for our Father cannot be fully loving unless the primal fear is acknowledged first. We cannot appreciate what we have outgrown if we have not first faced its existence. Benedict does not so much strike the fear of God into us as make us face the fear that is already there. He does this by commanding us to cultivate an awareness of God's presence. The second thing he wants us to learn from this fear is our own weakness and natural inability to please God without his grace.

From this understanding, Benedict leads us to the second rung of the ladder. He calls us to turn from our own will and guard our lives against all kinds of sin: "Moreover we ask God in our prayers that his will may be done in us . . . a man should not love his own will nor take pleasure in carrying out his desires . . . because death is stationed beside the entrance to delight."[13] Following our own desire is the way of pride. If our desires are tasteful and highbrow, they easily lead us into snobbery and pride. It is easy to look down our noses at the more sordid of our desires, but at least they keep us humble. Whether our desires are vulgar or refined, Benedict reminds us of God's presence in our lives and calls us to respond by doing God's will and not our own. It is submission to God's will that takes us from fear of God's punishment to an acceptance of his Love.

Thérèse submitted to God's will from an extraordinarily early age. On her deathbed she says, "From the age of three I have never denied God anything."[14] This natural obedience, combined with her own loving relationship with her earthly father, means there is scarcely a trace of the fear of God in Thérèse's writings. Instead "the good God" is her "Papa" and from the opening paragraph of her book she declares her theme, "I'm going to be doing only one thing: I shall begin to sing what I must sing eternally: 'the Mercies of the Lord.' "[15] By bypassing the fear of God Thérèse calls us immediately to leave fear behind and enter into the love of God. As little children we must be willing to do God's will and trust ourselves to his mercy. "Sanctity," she writes, "consists in a disposition of the heart that leaves us little and humble in God's arms, aware of our weakness and trusting unto folly in his fatherly goodness."[16]

Benedict's third step of humility "is that for the love of God one should be obedient to a superior in all things imitating the Lord of whom the Apostle says, 'He was made obedient even unto death.' "[17] Once more Benedict affirms the virtue of obedience and calls us to obey our religious superiors as Christ obeyed the Father. This is not just a command to help maintain order in the monastery or subservience in the monk. It applies to all Christians. All of us are subject to certain authorities and we grow far more by one small act of obedience than all our sincere and well-intentioned challenges to authority. Benedict sees that obedience and humility are interdependent as they were in Christ, and that through obedience, the ego-led personality is transformed into the image of Christ. Balthasar explains how it works:

> In his every word and deed, in all his miracles and suffering, the Son withdraws his 'personality' to let the will of the Father become manifest; his own personality appears only as the personification of obedience to the Father . . . the Lord demands that each person whom he calls to his intimate service should conform to this law. Each of them is given a position . . . which requires the withdrawal of his own personality behind the veil of pure objectivity and

obedience so that he may be poured into the saving stream of sacrifice that redeems the world.[18]

Benedict believes this identification with Christ is worked out through obedience to the proper religious authority. Balthasar observes how Thérèse fulfilled Benedict's ideal: "In obeying she loves the Lord himself; and therefore also loves . . . the person who represents that love to her: the Superior. She attends entirely and lovingly to the wishes of the Prioress, whether this is her own dear sister Pauline or the capricious Marie de Gonzague, whose moods were changeable as the weather."[19]

Thérèse writes to Marie de Gonzague: "Mother, you are the compass dear Jesus has provided to direct me safely to the eternal shore! How sweet it is for me to fix my gaze upon you and then carry out the will or our Lord! . . . (he) helps me to see in you not only a loving Mother but also Jesus living in your soul and communicating his will to me through you."[20]

Benedict's fourth step of humility deals with suffering:

> When in the very act of obeying one meets with trials, opposition and even abuse, a man should, with an uncomplaining spirit, keep a firm grip on patience, and as he endures he should neither grow faint nor run away; even as Scripture says, 'He who stands firm to the end will be saved' (Matt. 10.22) and again, 'Let your heart take courage and hope in the Lord' (Ps. 26.14).[21]

Benedict realizes that obedience will never lead to true humility until it is tested; likewise, Thérèse accepts suffering as part of her vocation in the convent. "A day without suffering in Carmel is a day lost,"[22] she writes, and like Benedict she encourages the novices in her charge to take courage and battle on: "Let us fight without ceasing, even without hope of winning the battle. What does success matter? Let us keep going, however exhausting the struggle may be! . . . one must do one's duty to the end."[23]

The battle is not simply a matter of being patient in the time of trial — hoping that things will get better. For both Benedict and Thérèse the suffering of obedience is intimately linked with the pursuit of humility, and as much as the suffering nurtures humility it leads to ultimate triumph. So Benedict says:

> Yet unmoved, through their hope of divine reward they joyfully persevere, saying, 'These are the trials through which we triumph on account of him who has loved us' (Rom.8.37). You tested us, O God; you refined us in the fire as silver is refined; you led us into the net; you laid tribulations on our backs (Ps. 65.10-11).[24]

Both Benedict and Thérèse realize that the terrible irony about the trials is that the loving superior they have promised to obey is actually the source of the trials. Benedict writes, "To show that we ought to be under a superior, the Scripture continues: 'You have set men over our heads' (Ps. 65.12)."[25] Although Thérèse wrote glowing words to Mother Marie de Gonzague, it was the same prioress who gave her a terrible time in the convent.

> Our Mother [Marie de Gonzague] who was often sick, had little time to spend with me. I knew she liked me very much and said everything good about me possible, yet God permitted her, without knowing it, to be very severe with me. I couldn't meet her without having to kiss the floor.[26]

Suffering does not necessarily nurture humility. It may only breed despair and bitterness. Only when it becomes part of

Christ's life and death can suffering merge into Christ's humility and bring the soul closer to sanctity. So Benedict links the suffering of obedience to the sacrifice of Christ: "To show us how a faithful man should suffer all things, however painful, on the Lord's behalf, Scripture gives voice to those who suffer in the words, 'For your sake we are afflicted by death all the day long and are reckoned as sheep for the slaughter' (Rom. 8.36)."[27]

Thérèse also saw her suffering as an identification with her Lord — the sacrificial Lamb. In her *Act of Oblation to Merciful Love* she writes:

> I thank You, O my God, for all the graces You have granted me, especially the grace of making me pass through the crucible of suffering. It is with joy I shall contemplate You on the Last Day carrying the sceptre of Your Cross. Since You deigned to give me a share in this very precious Cross, I hope in heaven to resemble You.[28]

The fifth step of humility for Benedict is to make a regular confession of sins: "A man should in humble confession reveal to his Abbot all the evil thoughts that come into his mind, and any wrongful actions that he has done in secret."[29] If the first step on the ladder of humility keeps the reality of God always before us, then this step keeps the reality of ourselves always before us. The reality of God and the reality of our own souls are a cause for both fear and praise: fear because we are so far from God's holiness, and praise because in confession our wrongs are put right. So Benedict says, " 'I have not covered up my evil actions; I made this resolve: I will confess my evil deeds and you have forgiven the guilt of my heart' (Ps. 31.5)."[30]

If the fourth rung that deals with suffering is grim, then this fifth step of the ladder of humility is a source of joy. One of the devil's greatest successes is to portray the sacrament of confession as an experience of doom, gloom, and guilt. Instead it is a sacrament of delight, forgiveness, and grace. Around the age of seven Thérèse made her first confession. She was properly prepared for the sacrament, and her response to the sacrament shows us the proper attitude to confession. She writes to her sister Pauline:

> Oh! Dear Mother, with what care you prepared me for my first confession, telling me it was not to a man but to God I was about to tell my sins; I was very much convinced of this truth. I made my confession in a great spirit of faith . . . coming out of the confessional I was so happy and light-hearted that I had never felt so much joy in my soul.[31]

When a Christian falls into sin, it should cause sorrow and a healthy form of guilt. When people deplore guilt, they mean unhealthy guilt — that neurotic mentality that blames oneself too much for failure and refuses to acknowledge the everlasting quality of God's forgiveness. Thérèse suffered from scruples, or extreme guilt, as a child, but it was replaced with supreme confidence in God's love. As a result her failures did not cause despair. They simply brought humility and realism about herself, and a fresh understanding of God's mercy. Thérèse realized that our sin is overwhelmed by God's love.

> Certainly every penance is laudable and meritorious if one is convinced that the good God requires it . . . but I could never bind myself to anything if it became a constant preoccupation . . . as our mother St. Teresa says: 'God is not concerned with a heap of trifles, as we too easily believe; and we should never let anything narrow our souls.'[32]

In our usual egocentric attitude we make the mistake that confession is all about our sinfulness when, in fact, it has far more to do with God's mercy. We might be keeping score, but God isn't. If men ought not to reckon, that is because God does not reckon, indeed cannot reckon because it would be contrary to his innermost essence, which is overflowing love. "There is one science he does not know," writes Thérèse, "— Arithmetic."[33]

The sixth step of humility "is that a monk should be satisfied with whatever is of lowest value or quality."[34] Benedict is not recommending poor quality on purpose; neither is he recommending a Franciscan vow of poverty. Instead he is recommending that poverty of spirit that does not worship material things. He also wants to take his sons past the fussiness and "tasteful" snobbery that is a form of pride. More than that, Benedict is pointing to a state of mind that is content with small sacrifices. Once again, Thérèse sums up Benedict's Rule in her life. So she writes, "I was taken up at this time with a real attraction for objects that were both very ugly and the least convenient. So it was with joy that I saw myself deprived of a pretty little jug in our cell and supplied with another large one, all chipped."[35]

She transforms her natural dislike for an ugly object into a spiritual growth point: "I applied myself to practising little virtues, not having the capability of practising the great."[36]

The monk's contentment with poor material objects must extend to his attitude to work as well: "With regard to the tasks laid on him he should think of himself as a bad and unworthy workman . . . 'I have been brought to nothing; I have known nothing; I am like a pack-animal before you' (Ps. 73.22)." If the monks' material things are poor offerings, so is even their best work. If they have great gifts, they should remember that they *are* gifts. If they have done their work well, then they are like the servants in

Luke 17:10 who, when they have completed their work, simply say, "We are only unworthy servants." Benedict realizes the attitude to work is important for the religious person. Pride in one's work may overtake anyone, but when one's work is religion, then ordinary pride is complicated by a spiritual dimension; thus spiritual pride lies waiting like a wolf at the door.

Thérèse echoes the same words of the unworthy servants from the Gospel. In the last days of her life she says, "Even if I had accomplished all the works of St. Paul, I would still believe myself to be a useless servant."[37] So far Thérèse echoes Benedict, who echoes the Gospel, but Thérèse sees that being an unworthy servant means relying utterly on God's grace; she continues, "It is precisely this that makes up my joy; for having nothing, I shall receive everything from God."[38] Balthasar sums it up:

> Her battle is to wipe out the hard core of Pharisaism that persists in the midst of Christianity; that human will-to-power disguised in the mantle of religion that drives one to assert one's own greatness instead of acknowledging that God alone is great.[39] . . . Thérèse does not sit in judgement on anyone's works or labors, but the one thing she cannot abide is that human beings should boast of their works in the face of God. To do so would be to insult grace.[40]

Thérèse undermines all self-righteousness with her simple humility: "It is to God alone that all value must be attributed; there's nothing of value in my little nothingness."[41]

The seventh step of humility in the Rule of St. Benedict is "that the monk should not only say in words that he is inferior and less virtuous than all other men, but that he should really believe it in the depth of his heart, making the same act of humility as the prophet who says, 'I am a worm and no man (Ps.

21.7) . . . . It is good that you have humiliated me, so that I may learn your commandments' (Ps. 118.71)."[42]

This passage of the Rule is almost comical in its recommendation of abject groveling. Furthermore, to tell someone to have such a lowly attitude toward himself is pointless; and here is the lesson underneath the lesson. At this point of his ladder of humility Benedict has shifted from prescription to description. He is not telling his monks to call themselves worms, but he is recognizing that the truly humble person really does believe himself to be the lowest of the low — in fact, that is the true fruit of his humility.

Thérèse expressed these very thoughts. She identifies herself as a grain of sand and writes, "Oh, how it desires to be reduced to nothing, unknown by any creature; poor little thing, it desires nothing more, nothing but to be forgotten . . . yes, I want to be forgotten, and not only by creatures, but also by myself."[43]

Blake saw eternity in a grain of sand, so it is when the saint is nothing that she can reveal everything. At the lowest point the highest peak is reached. In every great story the hero not only reaches the bottom of his resources, but he reaches what is called the "negation of the negation": a point of absolute zero where there is nothing left to lose. Only at that point is he able to rise and conquer.

Such utter humility can only be understood positively when seen with another metaphor that both Thérèse and Benedict use. Thérèse sees herself as an instrument in God's hands:

> If a piece of canvas painted by an artist could think
> and speak, it would certainly not complain at constantly
> being touched and retouched by the brush, and would
> not envy the lot of that instrument, for it would realise it

was not to the brush but to the artist using it that it owed the beauty with which it was clothed. The brush, too, would not be able to boast of the masterpiece produced with it, as it knows that artists are not at a loss; they play with difficulties, and are pleased to choose at times weak and defective instruments.[44]

Benedict says the instruments of the monastery must not be treated in "a dirty or careless manner."[45] An old monk once told me how, as a novice, he broke the leg of a fellow monk during rough games on the playing field. He was reprimanded by the novice master, "Brother, you have treated one of the instruments of the monastery in a dirty and careless manner!" So the humble soul may be likened to a worm or a grain of sand, but such a soul is also an instrument of the monastery, a paint brush in God's hands, a tool of grace that God will use as he sees fit.

Mother Teresa of Calcutta echoes her namesake when she points out how our being instruments is also a sign of God's humility:

> I find two things admirable: God's goodness and His humility. His love and His humility are striking. . . . He comes down to us and uses instruments as weak and imperfect as we are. He deigns to work through us. . . . We are not channels, we are instruments. Channels give nothing of their own, they just let the water run through them. In our actions we are instruments in God's hands. God writes through us and however imperfect instruments we may be, He writes beautifully.[46]

The eighth step on the ladder is that the monk should submit to the common rule of the monastery and the example of those above him. Thérèse fulfills this as she writes, "I have long since ceased to belong to myself. I have surrendered myself utterly to Jesus, so he is free to do with me as he pleases. . . . O my Mother, how much anxiety we are spared through taking the vow of obedience! How happy the simple religious, their sole compass being the will of their superiors."[47]

Once the individual is submerged in the community, the selfish good is caught up in the common good.

Benedict's ninth, tenth, and eleventh steps toward humility all deal with the need for sober silence.

> The monk should keep his tongue from talking; he should preserve silence . . . he should not be ready and quick to laughter . . . when a monk speaks, he does so quietly, without laughter, with humility, with restraint, making use of few words and reasonable ones, as it is written, 'The wise man becomes known for his few words.'[48]

Thérèse sees that one of the benefits of silence is that the person who doesn't say anything doesn't say anything uncharitable: "Take silence for example, what good it does to the soul, what failures in charity it prevents, and so many other troubles of so many kinds."[49]

At this point in his ladder of humility Benedict describes the essence of the monastic character. The spiritual person is silent because at heart he wants to spend time with God, and to do that he must withdraw from human conversation. He does not keep silent because he dislikes other humans, but because small talk is small. Chit-chat is to the life of prayer what static is to radio reception. The spiritual person's instinctive withdrawal alienates him from the mainstream and pushes him into a monastic isolation, whether he likes it or not. When she went to boarding school, Thérèse felt the tension her contemplative instincts caused.

> At the time of my First Communion I loved this
> association with children of my own age, filled with good
> will, having made like myself the resolution of practising virtue seriously, but now I had to come in contact
> with students who were much different, distracted and
> unwilling to observe regulations, and this made me very
> unhappy. I had a happy disposition, but I didn't know
> how to enter into games of my age level; often during
> the recreations, I leaned against a tree and studied my
> companions at a distance, giving myself up to serious
> reflections.[50]

Silence is the fruit of solitude, and the contemplative seeks
a secret place with the same compulsion the sinner seeks his den
of vice. Jesus was constantly going to a solitary place to pray and
he tells us to do the same (cf. Matthew 6:6). Benedict calls for
the oratory to be kept quiet so the monks may find a secret place
of prayer,[51] and as a child Thérèse instinctively sought out a private place for prayer.

> At this time in my life nobody had ever taught me
> how to make mental prayer, and yet I had a great desire to
> make it. . . . One day, one of my teachers . . . asked me
> what I did on my free afternoons when I was alone. I told
> her I went behind my bed in an empty space which was
> there, and that it was easy to close myself in with my bed
> curtain and that 'I thought.' 'But what do you think about?'
> she asked. 'I think about God, about life, about Eternity . . .
> I think!' . . . I understand now that I was making mental

prayer without knowing it and that God was already in-
structing me in secret.[52]

The silence that Benedict recommends is a paradoxical silence. The monk is silent, not because he is trying hard to keep
his mouth shut, but because what he has to say is both not worth
saying and too important to say. Compared to the mysteries he
has experienced, the mystic's own thoughts and words seem too
trivial to speak. At the same time, what he has seen is too far
beyond imagining to be put into words. Thus at the end of his
life, the great philosopher St. Thomas Aquinas had a mystical
experience that stunned him into silence, so he claimed that all
he had written was "straw" compared to what he had seen. Likewise, Thérèse relates her feelings about her first communion:

> The smallest details of that heavenly day have left
> unspeakable memories in my soul! . . . I don't want to en-
> ter into detail here. There are certain things that lose their
> perfume as soon as they are exposed to the air; there are
> deep spiritual thoughts which cannot be expressed in hu-
> man language without losing their intimate and heavenly
> meaning.[53]

Finally, Benedict's silence is a reflection of the hiddenness
of the humble soul. Humility never speaks its name. The humble
soul is hidden away. It is part of the Benedictine ethos to be
hidden in the enclosed monastery, but it is also the essence of
the Benedictine way to be hidden in the world like leaven in the
lump of dough (cf. Matthew 13:33). From this hidden position
Benedict's wisdom permeated the early Middle Ages, preserv-
ing ancient wisdom and laying the foundations for modern
Western culture. This active hiddenness is also one of Thérèse's

themes. She is Thérèse of the Holy Face, and so she wants to be hidden like the veiled face of Jesus: "Oh, I wished that my face, like the Face of Jesus, might be hidden from all glances, that no one on earth might know me any more."[54] She understands St. Paul, who says we are "hidden with Christ in God" (Colossians 3:3) and she knows her hiddenness means an intimate fusion with Christ. "Jesus is a hidden treasure, a good beyond price that few souls can find, for it is hidden. . . . To find a thing hidden, we must be hidden ourselves; so our life must be a mystery."[55] At the heart of this mystery the silent soul becomes a sacrament of Christ, hidden in the world and working her way into the world for the redemption of the world.

Benedict's final step seals the heart of humility: "The monk should be humble of heart, but also in his appearance his humility should be apparent to those who see him . . . and when all these steps of humility have been climbed the monk will soon reach that love of God which being perfect drives out all fear. Through this love all the practices which before he kept somewhat fearfully, he now begins to keep effortlessly and naturally and habitually."[56]

At this point humility has become part of the monk's character. The child in him has been reborn and he lives in a condition of "complete simplicity" that has cost "not less than everything."[57]

Benedict talks about the ladder of perfection, but Thérèse uses a different metaphor to teach how humility can really be accomplished. She says the quest is not one of climbing a ladder or a stairway at all. For Thérèse the ladder of perfection is too difficult and too legalistic. It requires too much self-analysis and human effort. She realizes she can't climb Benedict's ladder of perfection, so in one of her most famous images she prefers to take the lift (elevator):

Alas, I have always noticed, in comparing myself with the saints, the same difference between them and myself as we see between a mountain whose summit is lost in the clouds and an obscure little grain of sand trampled underfoot by passers-by. . . . It is impossible for me to grow great . . . but we live in an age of inventions; today there is no need to go to the trouble of climbing stairs; among rich people, an elevator has replaced the stairs; I also wished to discover an elevator to take me up to Jesus; because I am too little to climb the steep stairway of perfection.[58]

At the end Thérèse brings us back to the heart of Christian humility. The Christian soul is humble because she relies utterly on the grace of God:

When I think of the good God's statement: 'I shall come soon and bring my reward with me, repaying everyone according to his works,' then I say to myself that he will find himself very much embarrassed with me, because I have no works! So he will not be able to repay me according to my works. Very well, then, I trust that he will repay me according to his works.[59]

To rely on that grace is to rely on Jesus himself, and this is the essence of Christian humility. For Thérèse this humility is Truth. This insight is finally clarified in the agony of her deathbed. She sees clearly that humility and Truth are one, and that through humility we do not so much understand Truth as *experience* Truth. So with a terrible irony, at the climax of her crushing and terrible agony she affirms her grace-full humility, saying pitifully to her sisters, "Yes, it seems to me I never sought anything but the truth; yes, I have understood humility of heart . . . it seems to me I'm humble."[60]

At that point Thérèse was one with the crucified Christ, and all the rules and disciplines have only been vehicles to get her to that point. Benedict also realizes that his Rule is only a tool, and not an end in itself. At the end of his Rule he says of all the monastic writings, "What are these but aids to the attainment of virtue for good-living and obedient monks?"[61] The final goal is to live in the same unity with Christ that Thérèse proposes, for both Thérèse and Benedict believe that every Christian must eventually — in this life or in the life to come — reach the point of absolute zero where everything else fades in importance and they have learned in the depths of humility to "prefer nothing whatever to the love of Christ."[62]

Chapter Seven Endnotes

1. Quoted in John Clarke, O.C.D. (tr.), *St. Thérèse of Lisieux: Her Last Conversations,* Washington, D.C., ICS Publications, 1977, p. 16.
2. John Clarke, O.C.D. (tr.), *The Story of a Soul: The Autobiography of St. Thérèse of Lisieux,* Washington, D.C., ICS Publications, 1976, p. 15.
3. Abbot Parry (tr.), *The Rule of St. Benedict,* Leominster, Gracewing, 1997, p. 24.
4. Isaiah 66:12-13.
5. Cf. Genesis 28:12.
6. Parry, ibid.
7. Ibid.
8. Hans Urs Von Balthasar, *Two Sisters in the Spirit,* San Francisco, Ignatius Press, 1970, p. 245.
9. I. F. Görres, *The Hidden Face: A Study of St. Thérèse of Lisieux,* New York, Pantheon, 1959, p. 338.
10. Parry, p. 24.
11. Ibid., p. 25.
12. Proverbs 1:7.
13. Parry, p. 25.
14. Clarke, *[St. Thérèse's] Last Conversations,* p. 251.
15. Clarke, *The Story of a Soul,* p. 13.

16. Clarke, *[St. Thérèse's] Last Conversations*, p. 129.
17. Parry, p. 26.
18. Balthasar, pp. 149-150.
19. Ibid., p. 161.
20. Clarke, *The Story of a Soul*, p. 219.
21. Parry, pp. 26-27.
22. John Clarke, O.C.D. (tr.), *General Correspondence, Vol. I*, Washington, D.C., ICS Publications, 1988, p. 43.
23. Thomas N. Taylor (tr.), *Saint Thérèse of Lisieux, The Little Flower of Jesus*, New York, P. J. Kennedy, 1926, pp. 324-325.
24. Parry, p. 27.
25. Ibid.
26. Clarke, *The Story of a Soul*, p. 150.
27. Parry, p. 27.
28. Clarke, *The Story of a Soul*, p. 277.
29. Parry, p. 27.
30. Ibid., p. 28.
31. Clarke, *The Story of a Soul*, p. 41.
32. Görres, pp. 302-303.
33. Balthasar, p. 251.
34. Parry, p. 28.
35. Clarke, *The Story of a Soul*, p. 159.
36. Ibid.
37. Clarke, *[St. Thérèse's] Last Conversations*, p. 67.
38. Ibid.
39. Balthasar, p. 241.
40. Ibid., p. 256.
41. Clarke, *[St. Thérèse's] Last Conversations*, p. 141.
42. Parry, p. 28.
43. Clarke, *General Correspondence, Vol. I*, pp. 122-123.
44. Clarke, *The Story of a Soul*, p. 235.
45. Parry, p. 59.
46. E. Le Joly, S.J., *We Do It For Jesus — Mother Teresa*, London, Darton, Longman and Todd, 1977, pp. 180-181, quoted in Nelson, *Living the Little Way of Love*.
47. Clarke, *The Story of a Soul*, pp. 218-219.
48. Parry, pp. 28-29.
49. Clarke, *[St. Thérèse's] Last Conversations*, p. 137.
50. Clarke, *The Story of a Soul*, p. 81.
51. Parry, p. 82.
52. Clarke, *The Story of a Soul*, pp. 74-75.

53. Ibid., p. 77.
54. H. Petitot, O.P., *Saint Thérèse de Lisieux: Une Renaissance spirituelle,* Paris, Desclée, 1925, p. 105.
55. Clarke, *General Correspondence, Vol. II,* p. 809.
56. Parry, p. 29.
57. T. S. Eliot, *The Four Quartets,* London, Faber and Faber, 1986, p. 48.
58. Clarke, *The Story of a Soul,* pp. 207-208.
59. Clarke, *[St. Thérèse's] Last Conversations,* p. 43.
60. Ibid., p. 205.
61. Parry, p. 118.
62. Ibid., p. 116.

Eight

Order and
Wonder

Thoughts and Prayers

O come, let us worship and bow down, / let us kneel before the LORD, our Maker!

— PSALM 95:6

The heavens are telling the glory of God; / and the firmament proclaims his handiwork. / Day to day pours forth speech, / and night to night declares knowledge. / There is no speech, nor are there words; / their voice is not heard; / yet their voice goes out through all the earth, / and their words to the end of the world.

— PSALM 19:1-4

The silence of earth seemed to melt into the silence of the heavens. The mystery of earth was one with the mystery of the stars. . . . Aloysha felt clearly . . . that something firm and unshakeable as that vault of heaven had entered into his soul.

— DOSTOYEVSKY

The mystics of many religious traditions have spoken of the experience of the unity of all things. . . . In its extreme form the unity may be described as a loss of individuality and the joy as bliss or rapture.

— IAN BARBOUR

Prayer
May none of God's wonderful works keep silence; night or morning, bright stars, high mountains, the depths of the seas, sources of rushing rivers: may all these break into song as we sing to Father, Son and Holy Spirit. May all the angels in the heavens reply: Amen, Amen, Amen.

— ANONYMOUS, CIRCA THIRD TO SIXTH CENTURY

Henry Vaughan wrote: "I saw eternity the other night, / Like a great Ring of pure and endless light, / All calm, as it was bright."[1] Thérèse of Lisieux was similarly starry-eyed:

> When we were on the way home, I would gaze upon the stars that were twinkling ever so peacefully in the skies and the sight carried me away. There was especially one cluster of golden pearls that attracted my attention and gave me great joy because they were in the form of a 'T'. I pointed them out to Papa and told him my name was written in heaven.[2]

The poets and the children are right: with a sense of wonder they see past distinctions of fact or fiction to see both mystery and meaning not only in the stars but also in the whole world around them.

St. Benedict had a similar night vision. Gregory the Great recounts the story:

> Long before the Night Office began, the man of God was standing at this window, where he watched and prayed while the rest were still asleep. In the dead of night he suddenly beheld a flood of light shining down from above more brilliant than the sun, and with it every trace of darkness cleared away. Another remarkable sight followed. According to his own description, the whole world was gathered up before his eyes in what appeared to be a single ray of light.[3]

In his biography of St. Benedict, Gregory the Great writes, "There are two ways we can be carried out of ourselves. Either we fall *below* ourselves through sins of thought, or we are lifted *above* ourselves by the grace of contemplation."[4]

The contemplative cultivates a childlike wonder about all things. This freshness of mind is present in all the great saints, not only the mystics. Wonder is not the same thing as curiosity. Monkeys and cats are curious, but they are not full of wonder. Curiosity demands an answer, but wonder gazes at the Truth. Curiosity is concerned with facts, wonder is concerned with meaning; curiosity is restless, wonder is at peace.

Although they appear similar, Christian contemplation is different from the meditation of Eastern religions. A Buddhist monk sees through everything, while the Christian monk looks through all things. In other words, the Buddhist tries to see through the illusion of created things to the void beyond, while the Christian uses the created world as an icon — looking through it to the Creator beyond. For the Christian contemplative all created things surge with the grandeur of God; he shares with the poet, the child, and the saint the eyes to see what Hopkins called the "dearest freshness deep down things."[5]

At the heart of Christian contemplation is a sense of wonder that is based on the realization that there is a pattern and meaning woven into the very fabric of the cosmos. Thérèse was filled with wonder at the immensity of the night sky, but she was *thrilled* with wonder when she traced her initials there. Wonder is therefore tied up with order. Without order in the universe, there is no wonder. Chaos only inspires confusion. For the poet Vaughan wonder and order depend on one another, for immediately following his sense of wonder at seeing eternity like "a great Ring of pure and endless light" he senses the order of the universe:

And round beneath it, Time, in hours, days, years,
Driven by the spheres

Like a vast shadow moved, in which the world
And all her train were hurled.[6]

The instinct to seek both order and wonder is present in Benedict and Thérèse. From childhood onward, they understand that for the wonder to be maintained, order must be imposed. One of the reasons Benedict insists on the monk living in community, and why Thérèse was so eager to join the community at Carmel, is so that the discipline of community life can provide the order necessary for the contemplative life to expand. Thérèse provides a homely metaphor for the interplay of order and wonder in the religious life. After she is enthralled by the stars she asks her father to guide her so she can continue to contemplate their beauty. "I pointed them out to Papa . . . then desiring no longer to look upon this dull earth, I asked him to guide my steps; and not looking where I placed my feet I threw back my head, giving myself over completely to the contemplation of the star-studded firmament!"[7] Similarly, Father Benedict's Rule guides his sons so that they can be free to contemplate the mysteries of heaven.

Benedict guides his sons with the same surefooted gentleness that M. Martin must have guided Thérèse. In the Prologue he encourages them by saying, "We propose, therefore to establish a school for the Lord's service, and in setting it up we hope we shall lay down nothing that is harsh or hard to bear."[8] Benedict is gentle but not soft. The tempered strictness of the Rule is there so that the monk will not "be overcome with terror, and run away from the way of salvation."[9] In his instructions to the abbot, Benedict says he must adapt his method to the needs and personalities of each of his charges. "He must show the tough attitude of a master, and also the loving affection of a father."[10] The goal of Benedict's discipline is to open his sons' hearts to

God through a life of contemplation. He wants their hearts to be like the cloister garden at the heart of their abbey — enclosed on every side, but open to the heavens.

Benedict establishes the necessary order through the vows of stability and obedience, but order alone cannot cultivate wonder. Like any gift, contemplation must be understood, developed, and practiced. It not only needs discipline and order, it also needs constant nourishment and practice. Without some other inspiration the discipline of the monastery would smother that fragile wonder that lies at the center of the contemplative heart. Outward order helps channel the inward vision, but the heart and mind need to be fed from other sources for wonder to be nurtured. Benedict therefore establishes *lectio divina*, or prayerful reading, as the inspiration for the inner life. In prayerful reading the contemplative soul experiences the wonder of God's handiwork and the order that gives it meaning.

In chapter forty-eight Benedict outlines the number of hours to be spent in prayerful reading. He includes these instructions in a chapter devoted to the daily manual labor, and in another chapter he calls the divine office the work of God. His point is that prayerful reading, like the liturgy and manual work, is a kind of prayer. Benedict's *lectio divina* does not consist of random spiritual writings. The primary source for prayerful reading is the Sacred Scriptures. In addition he recommends the classics of the monastic life: the lives of the Desert Fathers, the *Conferences* and *Institutes* of John Cassian, and the Rule of St. Basil.

Prayerful reading is not speed-reading. Our modern technique of reading matches the shallowness of most of the content we read. With so much verbiage thrust at us every day, we skim, jumping from article to article and skipping to the end once our interest has waned. Prayerful reading requires a different technique, one that is suitable for the profound content being read. Prayerful reading is a discipline similar to careful listening. For *lectio divina* to succeed, the reader has to slow down, allowing time for God's word to sink in and for the Truth to take root within the heart.

Reading silently is a fairly modern skill. In the past, reading was almost always done aloud. St. Augustine was amazed when he discovered that St. Ambrose could read silently. Dom Jean Leclercq describes the ancient technique of reading, "In the Middle Ages, as in antiquity, they read usually, not as today principally with the eyes, but with the lips, pronouncing what they saw, and with the ears, listening to the words pronounced, hearing what is called, the 'voices of the pages.' "[11] They read slowly, taking time to think through the text and allowing their thoughts to merge into prayer. This kind of meditation is a constant interplay between the objective text and the subjective reactions to it. Because it is Scripture-based, Christian meditation always has a physical and historical element. The Bible is the story of God's relationship with real historical characters. Reading aloud strengthens the physical and temporal aspect of meditation because as the reader speaks and listens to the words they become real sounds and occupy real time in his experience.

In addition to reading aloud, Benedict's prayerful reading included memorization. So Benedict gives the monks time to memorize, exhorting them that "the time that is left after Matins is to be used for further study by the brethren whose knowledge of the Psalter or of the readings is incomplete."[12] The Psalms are especially memorable, since they speak from the heart of the psalmist to the heart of the human condition. John Cassian recounts how his mentor Abbot Nesteros encouraged the whole of Scripture to be memorized:

> Give yourself over assiduously, or rather continuously to sacred reading, until continual meditation fills your heart and fashions you so to speak after its own likeness . . . the whole series of the Holy Scriptures should be diligently committed to memory and ceaselessly repeated.[13]

Memorization allows the words of Scripture to enter the deepest level of the human memory and consciousness. The New Testament says the "Word of God is sharper than a two-edged sword, penetrating even to the soul and spirit."[14] As the Word of God is memorized, it renews the mind, allowing the deep sources of imagination to be nourished so that contemplative wonder is renewed.

The point of *lectio divina* is to bring the soul into a closer experience of God. As Wulfstan Mork puts it, "The study of a text in *lectio divina,* pursuing its meaning, was not done for the sake of knowing about God, but of knowing God by experience, contacting him in his Word."[15] Prayerful reading is a form of prayer that leads through mental meditation to spiritual contemplation. Guigo the Carthusian wrote, "It is as the Lord says, 'Seek and you shall find; knock and it shall be opened to you' (Matt. 7.7)." Seek in reading and you will find in meditating; knock in praying and you shall enter through contemplation."[16] The contemplation that follows is a wordless dwelling in the reality of God's presence. In T. S. Eliot's words it is "the still point of the turning world, / Neither flesh nor fleshless; / Neither from nor toward, there the dance is . . . a grace of sense, a white light still and moving."[17]

Benedict's monks were immersed in Scripture, and Thérèse's life followed the same pattern. Early in her life she was inseparable from *The Imitation of Christ,* and she confided: "I knew almost all the chapters of my beloved *Imitation* by heart. This little book never parted company with me."[18] She also read extensively in the other spiritual writings so that her novice mistress was astounded at her knowledge of St. John of the Cross.[19] Eventually other spiritual books paled in significance to Sacred Scripture.

> If I open a book by a spiritual author (even the most beautiful, the most touching book) I feel my heart contract immediately and I read without understanding, so to speak. Or if I do understand, my mind comes to a standstill without the capacity of meditating. In this helplessness, Holy Scripture and the *Imitation* come to my aid; in them I discover a solid and very pure nourishment. But it is especially the Gospels that sustain me during my hours of prayer. . . . I am constantly discovering in them new lights, hidden and mysterious meanings.[20]

She points this out, as she had read St. John of the Cross and memorized much of the *Imitation of Christ*. Most of all Thérèse memorized the Scriptures.

> The novices whom she instructed tell of how she used at all times to amaze them by her display of scriptural knowledge. She always carried a copy of the New Testament around with her. In her cell, she used to write out passages and work out a sort of concordance of her own.[21]

Like Benedict, her writings are sprinkled generously with quotations from the Scriptures showing a capacity to quote by memory great portions of the Psalms and both Testaments. One of her sisters recounts, "Quotations from the Gospels used to come pouring out whenever she wished to drive home something she was telling me. She seemed to know them by heart."[22]

Thérèse takes the importance of Scripture to its final conclusion. Since the Scriptures are the Word of God she does not need to rely on extravagant learning and the mastery of esoteric texts of spirituality. As she has taken the lift of God's grace rather than climb the ladder of perfection, so she will also use the simplicity and profundity of Scripture as a lift: "I looked for the desired elevator in the Sacred Scriptures and found the words coming from the mouth of the Eternal Wisdom, 'Whoever is a little one let him come to me' (Prov. 9.4)."[23] For both Benedict and Thérèse the Scriptures are "the words of eternal life"[24] and as such they are like a fountain springing up within their hearts and minds.[25] Reading the Scriptures leads them from meditating on God into a contemplative experience of God's love. This contemplative action is at the heart of the childlike wonder that Benedict encourages and that Thérèse retains throughout her life.

To nurture a contemplative spirit through meditative reading is one thing. To seek mystical experiences in order to relieve a religious life that seems dull is another. If some sort of mystic vision is given, then it is a glimpse of the goal, but not the goal itself. To pursue a vision or a moment of wonder is an attempt to reach the destination without having made the journey. It substitutes a film about the ascent of Everest for climbing the mountain. Those who chase such ephemeral things will either be disappointed or end up worshiping devils who promise delights. The moments of wonder or mystical insight do not last because God wishes for us to experience something better. It is the Christian way to discover his grace not in the heights of mystical experience but in the depths of ordinary existence.

Along with her moments of wonder Thérèse had certain mystical experiences. She believed she had been healed, and she believed she had seen the Virgin Mary smile. She described a mystic piercing of Love similar to Teresa of Ávila's: "I had commenced the Way of the Cross, when I felt myself suddenly wounded by a dart of fire so ardent that I thought I must die . . . an invisible power seemed to plunge me wholly into the fire . . . but oh! What fire! What sweetness!"[26]

Despite her extraordinary experiences, Thérèse has no time for mystical delights or visions. She is quite sure Christ is to be found in her ordinary life and in her extraordinary sufferings. She says to her sister, "I have no wish to go to Lourdes to have ecstasies. I prefer the monotony of sacrifice."[27] In her submission to the dull routine of life Thérèse felt she was emulating the Mother of God; so she says, "I know, O Mother full of grace, that you lived in great poverty in Nazareth. You did not long to leave it; no raptures, miracles or ecstasies lightened your life . . . you chose to tread the everyday paths so as to show little ones the way to heaven."[28]

For all the accounts of miracles and visions in the legends about Benedict, he never mentions mystical prayer. Instead his Rule deals with the ordinary nuts and bolts of the monk's life. Benedict specifies that psalms are to be sung, when the offices are to be said, and how to vary them according to the different hours of daylight. Benedict's detailed ordering of the monastic worship is, for most people, the dullest part of the Rule, and yet it is this mundane attention to detail that Benedict considers important.

Mystical experiences may inspire and lift prayer, but order is established through the regular recitation of the liturgy. In the liturgy Thérèse and Benedict express their deep love of God in a daily, formal routine. The regular offices and the rhythm of the liturgical year are the heartbeat of the religious life. Benedict gives detailed instructions for the proper recitation of the liturgy, and Thérèse expresses a similar attention to liturgical detail:

> How proud I was when I was hebdomadarian [the nun who presides at the office] during the recitation of the Divine Office. . . . I had a great desire to recite it well, without making any mistakes. . . . I don't believe that one could have had a greater desire to recite the Office more perfectly than I and to be present in choir.[29]

The heart of liturgy beats, but the heart is also the center of love and passion. As order is balanced by wonder, the formal prayer of the Divine Office is balanced by the spontaneous and loving prayer of the heart. Both Benedict and Thérèse recommend intimate, childlike prayer. Jesus and St. Paul teach us to call God "Papa." The same childlike prayer is recommended by Benedict and Thérèse. Benedict says the oratory should be kept as a place of silence and reverence so that anyone may enter there to pray with the "attention of the heart."[30] Prayers are never to be ornate or lengthy. Instead we must grasp that "it is not by using many words that we shall get our prayers answered, but by purity of heart and repentance with tears. Prayer should therefore be short and pure."[31]

Benedict's advice that prayer must be offered with "purity of heart" sums up his attitude to personal prayer. Columba Cary-Elwes points out that " 'purity of heart' is the translation for the Greek word *apatheia*. . . . Its original pagan meaning was 'detachment'; without feeling, a state of insensibility, coldness. The Christians took the word over from the Greeks, the Stoics and others . . . but the primary attitude of a Christian in prayer is not non-attachment. It is a firm deep longing or attachment

(love) with all our hearts, minds, strength and all our being, for
God. John Cassian . . . had the great wisdom . . . to translate
apatheia into 'purity of heart.' "[32]
Therefore at the core of Benedict's prayer is not formal detachment or liturgical routine, but a deep longing for God that
is expressed in simple brevity.
Thérèse also has no time for elaborate prayers:

> It's a mistake to imagine that your prayer won't be
> answered unless you've something out of a book, some
> splendid formula of words. . . . If that were true I'm afraid
> I should be in a terribly bad position. . . . I can't face the
> strain of hunting about in books for these splendid prayers
> — it makes my head spin. There are such a lot of them,
> each more splendid than the last; how am I to recite them
> all, or to choose between them? I just do what children
> have to do before they've learnt to read, I tell God what I
> want quite simply, without any splendid turns of phrase,
> and somehow he always manages to understand me. For
> me, prayer means a launching out of the heart towards
> God; it means lifting up one's eyes, quite simply to heaven,
> a cry of grateful love, from the crest of joy or the trough of
> despair, it's a vast supernatural force which opens out my
> heart and binds me close to Jesus.[33]

The routine of the daily liturgy is balanced by, and inter-
weaves with, the intimate prayer of the heart. The two forms of
prayer are vital for every Christian. The formal worship of the
Church is empty ritualism without a fervent life of spontaneous
prayer of the heart. On the other hand, freelance worship that is
driven only by subjective feelings is both ephemeral and pedes-
trian. Together, a life of prayer can be constructed that equips

every man and woman to deal with the joys and sorrows of daily life. From this balance of prayer, Scripture, and liturgy, the ordinary life can open out into a life of contemplation.

This contemplation is not some lofty, transcendent religious experience. As the "conversion experience" must be forged into conversion of life, so the "contemplative moment" must be forged into a contemplative life. This means viewing life with "sacramental eyes." Such a life is not "ordinary" life plastered over with a few religious duties, nor is it a sentimental attempt to see "meaning" in every event. Instead the contemplative life is infused with the awareness that every moment is charged with the grandeur of God. This simple life is openhearted, looking for the best in all things because all things have been given by the loving Father. It is a life in which wonder and order are woven together so that eternity is alive in every moment.

This new kind of awareness is like waking up from sleep. So at the beginning of the Rule Benedict says, "Let us then at last arouse ourselves, even as Scripture incites us in the words, 'Now is the hour for us to rise from sleep.' Let us, then, open our eyes to the divine light, and hear with our ears the divine voice as it cries out to us daily."[34]

The contemplative soul is awake and alert. She is watchful like the virgins in the Gospel who are looking for the bridegroom (cf. Matthew 25). Benedict often weaves spiritual meaning into mundane matters, so in his instructions on how the monks should sleep he teaches a lesson about a sleepy spirit as opposed to contemplative watchfulness. Alluding to the Gospel about the watchful virgins he says:

> A candle should burn continuously in the room until morning. They should sleep clothed, girt with girdles or cords. . . . And so let the monks always be ready and when

the signal is given they should get up without delay and make as to arrive first for the Work of God.[35]

In a homely detail he echoes the Gospel again: just as the virgins encouraged one another on the way to meet the bridegroom, so "when they get up for the Work of God they may quietly encourage one another since the sleepy are given to making excuses."[36] In Benedict's time the office of Matins took place in the wee hours of the morning. Because the monks arose in the middle of the night to watch and pray, the Night Office was an identification with the watchful virgins of the Gospel and an embodiment of the watchful spirit. This watchfulness for God is at the heart of the contemplative life, and its purpose is not only to reveal God's mighty acts in all his works, but to discover his action in our own lives.

Thérèse always personalizes the Truth. What is true must be alive in her experience. So to see God at work in all things and in every moment means God must be alive in the depths of our own hearts. To see God really and truly present — there is the final test for the contemplative spirit. Knowing Christ within as her spiritual director par excellence, Thérèse writes:

> I understand and I know from experience that the 'Kingdom of God is within you.' Jesus has no need of books or teachers to instruct souls; He teaches without the noise of words. Never have I heard Him speak, but I feel that He is within me at each moment; He is guiding and inspiring me with what I must say and do.[37]

The final goal of the contemplative life is seeing the incarnation not as a dull doctrine or a historical fact but as a dynamic event in the present moment. It is developing the vision to see that God is working out his will and his way not only among the stars, but within our ordinary lives. Through his Spirit the resurrected Lord is surging in and through the most mundane matters of life, and therefore within our own hearts. The contemplative comes to see and experience this action of God, and then she responds with praise. So Benedict says, "We believe that God is present everywhere and that the eyes of the Lord are in every place . . . but most of all we should believe this without any shadow of doubt, when we are engaged in the Work of God . . . we should therefore . . . sing wisely."[38]

Thérèse joins in the song, saying in the first sentence of her book, "I shall be doing only one thing: I shall begin to sing what I must sing eternally: 'The mercies of the Lord.' "[39]

Chapter Eight Endnotes

1. Henry Vaughan, "The World," in *The Faber Book of Religious Verse*, ed. Helen Gardner, London, Faber and Faber, 1972, p. 175.

2. John Clarke, O.C.D. (tr.), *The Story of a Soul: The Autobiography of St. Thérèse of Lisieux*, Washington, D.C., ICS Publications, 1976, p. 43.

3. Odo Zimmerman, O.S.B., and Benedict Avery, O.S.B. (tr.), *Life and Miracles of St. Benedict* (Book II of the *Dialogues*), Prologue, Collegeville, Minnesota, The Liturgical Press, 1987, p. 35.

4. Ibid., p. 3.

5. Gerard Manley Hopkins, "God's Grandeur," in *The Faber Book of Religious Verse*, ed. Helen Gardner, London, Faber and Faber, 1972, p. 288.

6. Vaughan, "The World," in *The Faber Book of Religious Verse*, p. 175.

7. Clarke, *The Story of a Soul*, p. 43.

8. Abbot Parry (tr.), *The Rule of St. Benedict*, Leominster, Gracewing, 1997, p. 4.

9. Ibid.

10. Ibid., p. 13.

11. Wulstan Mork, O.S.B., *The Benedictine Way*, Petersham, St. Bede's Publications, 1987, p. 32.

12. Parry, p. 30.

13. John Cassian, *Conferences*, in Edgar C. S. Gibson (tr.), *Nicene and Post-Nicene Fathers*, Grand Rapids, Michigan, William Eerdmans, 1964, p. 440, quoted in Mork, p. 33.
14. Hebrews 4:12.
15. Mork, p. 34.
16. Maurus Wolter, O.S.B., *The Principles of Monasticism*, St. Louis, Herder Book Co., 1962, p. 215. Quoted in Mork, p. 35.
17. T. S. Eliot, *The Four Quartets*, London, Faber and Faber, 1986, p. 15.
18. Clarke, *The Story of a Soul*, p. 102.
19. H. Petitot, O.P., *Saint Thérèse de Lisieux: Une Renaissance spirituelle*, Paris, Desclée, 1925, p. 69.
20. Clarke, *The Story of a Soul*, p. 179.
21. Hans Urs Von Balthasar, *Two Sisters in the Spirit*, San Francisco, Ignatius Press, 1970, p. 83.
22. Petitot, p. 72.
23. Clarke, *The Story of a Soul*, pp. 207-208.
24. Cf. John 6:68.
25. Cf. John 4:14.
26. Clarke, *[St. Thérèse's] Last Conversations*, p. 77.
27. John Clarke, O.C.D. (tr.), *General Correspondence, Vol. I*, Washington, D.C., ICS Publications, 1988, p. 620.
28. From a poem by Thérèse, quoted by Balthasar, p. 337.
29. Clarke, *[St. Thérèse's] Last Conversations*, pp. 137-138.
30. Parry, p. 82.
31. Ibid., p. 43.
32. Columba Cary-Elwes, O.S.B., *Work and Prayer, the Rule of St. Benedict for Lay People*, Tunbridge Wells, Burns and Oates, 1992, p. 77.
33. Ronald Knox (tr.), *Autobiography of a Saint*, London, Collins, 1973, p. 228.
34. Parry, p. 1.
35. Ibid., p. 45.
36. Ibid.
37. Clarke, *The Story of a Soul*, p. 179.
38. Parry, p. 42.
39. Clarke, *The Story of a Soul*, p. 13.

.

Nine

Embracing
All Things

Thoughts and Prayers

The earth is the LORD's and the fulness thereof, / the world and those who dwell therein.

— PSALM 24:1

For all things are yours, . . . the world or life or death or the present or the future, all are yours; and you are Christ's; and Christ is God's.

— 1 CORINTHIANS 3:21-23

A man is most often right in what he affirms and wrong in what he denies.

— F. D. MAURICE

Can you be righteous unless you be just in rendering to things their due esteem? All things were made to be yours and you were made to prize them according to their value.

— THOMAS TRAHERNE

Mine are the heavens and mine is the earth; mine are the people, the righteous are mine and mine are the sinners; the angels are mine and the Mother of God, and all things are mine, and God himself is mine and for me, for Christ is mine and all for me. What, then, dost thou ask for and seek, my soul? Thine is all this, and it is all for thee.

— ST. JOHN OF THE CROSS

Prayer
I will have all.

— THÉRÈSE OF LISIEUX

Thérèse was enthralled by the stars, but she did not seek to be a "star." She would have understood that the famous "stars" of the world are mere comets that flash across the sky only to vanish and be forgotten. Stars usually seek their own stardom and their ephemeral fame is their only sad achievement. Thérèse stands these worldly pursuits on their head: she has become universally famous by devoting her life to remaining anonymous. She has become well known for being unknown and has inherited everything by forfeiting everything. Her subsequent stardom is both a paradox and a providential practical joke. It is the sort of chicanery she would have enjoyed immensely.

The nuns who knew her testified that during her lifetime Thérèse did not seem remarkable in any way. "Hundreds, thousands of nuns had lived similar lives, good, pure, devout; there was nothing to distinguish Sister Thérèse from their long procession."[1] Vita Sackville-West compares her to another Carmelite nun, Beatriz Oñez, who was professed in 1570 in Valladolid:

> She was said never to utter a word with which fault could be found: never known to make an excuse for herself. . . . She never complained, never failed in obedience but did whatever she was commanded to do readily, perfectly and with joy. The most trifling thing we do, she was wont to say, is beyond all price if we do it for the love of God.[2]

She went on to ask God for suffering in order to identify with Christ; then, like Thérèse, she hid the suffering when it came. She died in the same mixture of agony and ecstasy, and "as her body was laid in the tomb a most powerful and sweet smell was perceived arising from it. Yet, for all the similarity what honour has ever been paid on earth to Beatriz Oñez?"[3]

When the nuns of Lisieux printed Thérèse's little book, her mission on earth exploded like the birth of a new star. The book was first read in convents, then lent to friends. The Carmel at Lisieux was soon inundated with orders for *The Story of a Soul*. Before long the convent was besieged with young women from all over the world who wanted to come and emulate Thérèse. Stories of miraculous cures and conversions began to flood into Carmel: A Scottish Presbyterian minister was converted to the Catholic faith and went to live in Thérèse's birthplace at Alençon to manage the increasing correspondence. A hard-bitten factory owner in Liverpool read the *Story of a Soul* and ordered a statue of Thérèse to be placed in all his workshops, gave copies of the book to his people, and gave them a week's holiday with full pay. A young seminarian in Bayeux was healed, as was a bishop in Upper Congo. In the United States, doctors and nurses advised patients to invoke her aid; and the Lisieux Carmel was flooded with requests from all over the world for relics and portraits of Thérèse. By 1923 the Carmel at Lisieux was receiving between eight hundred and a thousand letters every day. In 1925 — just twenty-eight years after Thérèse's death — St. Peter's Square was crowded with over five hundred thousand people to celebrate her canonization. Maurice de Waleffe, a skeptical journalist, wrote in *Le Journal* that "the world had fallen on its knees before the purest soul since Francis of Assisi."[4]

Thérèse of Lisieux's rise to fame is so extraordinary that it must be a sign of God's hand at work. Pope Pius XI recognized God's power working through the life of little Thérèse. At the ceremony of her beatification he said:

> The voice of God and the voice of his people have joined in extolling the Venerable Thérèse of the Child Jesus. The voice of God first made itself heard, and the faithful recog-

nising the divine call, added their voices to the anthem of praise. We repeat, the voice of God was the first to speak.[5]

As Balthasar has said, hers is one of those missions that "flash across the dome of the Church like lightning from heaven and light up unmistakably some unique point of God's will for the Church."[6]

At every point Thérèse followed her own teaching of being totally hidden in humility. In the evidence given at the proceedings for her canonization it became clear that all her writing was done not out of desire to be known, but in religious obedience to her superiors. Balthasar says, "Originally she herself never dreamed that she might be chosen to bear some fundamental message to the Church."[7] Only in the last days of her life did she suddenly realize how her work would be used by God in a universal mission.

> She became aware of it only gradually; in fact, it did not occur to her until her task was almost completed, after she had already lived out her teaching and was writing the last chapters of her book. Suddenly as she saw it all laid out before her, she recognized its strangeness, that in her obedience she had unwillingly conceived something beyond her own personality.[8]

At the end she realized the grace she had been given was like the mustard seed that grows into the largest tree. "I'm a little seed; no one knows yet what will develop."[9] She knew how important her little life would become, saying, "All the world will love me."[10] She knew how important her little book would become, warning her sister to take care with the publication and saying that her writings would "do a great deal of good."[11] On her deathbed she realized her universal mission was just beginning: "I feel that my mission will soon begin — to teach souls to love God as I love him, to give them my 'little way.' If my wishes are realized I shall spend my heaven on earth until the end of the world."[12] At the end of her life she writes, "I want to be a daughter of the Church . . . and to pray for the Holy Father's intentions which I know embrace the whole universe."[13] She knew, too, that her doctrine would become universally admired, and Balthasar clarifies the role she plays in the Church:

> Her life contains exemplary value for the Church in-
> sofar as the Holy Spirit possessed her and used her in or-
> der to demonstrate something for the sake of the Church,
> opening up new vistas onto the Gospels. That, and that
> alone, should be the motive for the Church's interest in
> Thérèse.[14]

That her mission is universal was recognized by Pope Benedict XV. In his speech upholding Thérèse's heroic practice of Christian virtue he says, "It is our special desire that the secret of her sanctity may be disclosed to all our children. . . . The more the knowledge of this new heroine is spread abroad, the greater will be the number of her imitators giving glory to God by the practice of the virtues of spiritual childhood."[15]

That her mission has spread to every corner of the globe and continues to spread is a fact that supports the divine inspiration of her life and work. It is also a confirmation of her own insights into the nature of God's calling in her life.

The seed of her universal mission is contained in a story from Thérèse's childhood:

> One day Léonie, thinking she was too big to be playing
> any longer with dolls, came to us with a basket filled with

dresses and pretty pieces for making others; her doll was resting on top. 'Here, my little sisters, choose; I'm giving you all this.' Céline stretched out her hand and took a little ball of wool that pleased her. After a moment's reflection, I stretched out mine saying: 'I choose all!' and I took the basket without further ceremony. Those who witnessed the scene saw nothing wrong and even Céline herself didn't dream of complaining. . . . This little incident of my childhood is a summary of my whole life; later on when perfection was set before me, I understood that to become a saint one had to suffer much. . . . Then, as in the days of my childhood, I cried out: 'My God, I choose all! I don't want to be a saint by halves . . . I choose all that You will!'[16]

This theme of "choosing all" recurs throughout her life and teachings. In choosing all, Thérèse wishes to embrace every detail of God and his creation. Her universal mission is the fruit of her ability to embrace all things through the contemplative life. Thérèse's character was contemplative by nature, and through contemplation she entered into a covenant of love with all creation. She recounts how, when her father took her on a fishing trip, she drifted into the reverie of the contemplative: she would sit on a little blossoming meadow just apart from her father, "Then my thoughts would become very deep; and without knowing what meditation meant, my soul became absorbed in true prayer. I would listen to distant sounds, the murmur of the wind, and so forth. Sometimes indistinct notes of military music reached me where I was and filled my heart with gentle melancholy. The earth seemed to be a place of exile, and I dreamed only of heaven."[17]

Her wish to embrace all the beauties of the earth shines in the account of her travels to Rome: "First there was Switzerland with its mountains whose summits were lost in the clouds, its graceful waterfalls gushing forth in a thousand different ways, its deep valleys literally covered with gigantic ferns and scarlet heather . . . how much good these beauties of nature poured out in such profusion did my soul!"[18]

All the glorious scenery is for Thérèse something to be "seen with the heart." It is a foretaste of heaven itself and she will take this vision of the whole world with her into the narrow confines of the convent. Reflecting on what she had seen she writes:

> The religious life appeared to me exactly as it is with all its subjections, its small sacrifices carried out in the shadows. I understood how easy it is to become all wrapped up in self, forgetting entirely the sublime goal of one's calling. I said to myself: 'When I am a prisoner in Carmel and trials come my way and I have only a tiny bit of the starry heavens to contemplate, I shall remember what my eyes have seen today. This thought will encourage me and I shall easily forget my own little interests, recalling the grandeur and power of God. . . . I will not have the misfortune of snatching after straws now that my heart has an idea of what Jesus has reserved for those who love him.'[19]

Thérèse is also eager to embrace the marvelous works of human genius she sees on her journey:

> After considering the power of Almighty God, I had the opportunity of admiring the power He has bestowed on His creatures. The first Italian city we visited was Milan. We examined minutely its white marble cathedral. . . . We climbed up to the lower pinnacles adorning the roof of the cathedral, and leaving some timid ladies to hide their faces we reached the top of the marble bell tower.[20]

She recounts her journey through Italy with great zest, taking everything in and embracing it all as God's gift to his child: "I was acting toward Him like a child who believes everything is permitted and looks upon the treasures of its Father as its own."[21]

If Thérèse embraces the beauties of nature and the wonders of human art and architecture as her own, she is even more expansive in her desire to embrace everything the Christian calling has to offer. In meditating on her vocation she knows her place but longs for much more:

> To be Your Spouse, to be a Carmelite, and by my union with You to be the Mother of souls, should not this suffice me? And yet it is not so. No doubt, these three privileges sum up my true vocation . . . and yet I feel within me other vocations. I feel the vocation of the Warrior, the Priest, the Apostle, the Doctor, the Martyr. Finally, I feel the need and the desire of carrying out the most heroic deeds for You, O Jesus.[22]

She had been taught that "the zeal of a Carmelite embraces the whole world,"[23] and so with missionary zeal she declares:

> In spite of my littleness, I would like to enlighten souls as did the Prophets and the Doctors. I have the vocation of the Apostle. I would like to travel over the whole earth to preach Your Name and to plant Your glorious cross on infidel soil. But . . . one mission alone would not be sufficient for me, I would want to preach the Gospel on all the five continents simultaneously and even to the most remote isles. I would be a missionary, not for a few years only, but from the beginning of creation until the consummation of the ages.[24]

Thérèse's desire to be a missionary is partially fulfilled in the lives of the countless missionaries, priests, and religious who have been inspired by her life and writings. Not least of these missionaries is Mother Teresa of Calcutta, who took her name from Thérèse, and based her own spirituality and the spirituality of her nuns on the teachings of Thérèse. Indeed the name "Missionary of Charity" sums up Thérèse's whole calling. Within the whole Church the cosmic vocation of Thérèse is fulfilled more completely and literally than she could ever have imagined.

Thérèse also believes her contemplative vocation is a way of being a missionary. She was given two missionary priests to pray for and write to, and in them she sees her own missionary vocation being fulfilled. With her usual quick wit she writes to one of them:

> Let us work together for the salvation of souls; I of course, can do very little, absolutely nothing, in fact, alone; what encourages me is the thought that by your side I can be of some use; after all, zero by itself has no value, but put alongside one, it becomes potent, always provided it is put on the proper side, after and not before. . . . So please, Brother, be good enough to send your blessing to the little zero the good God has put beside you![25]

Thérèse is sometimes kidnapped by those who press for women's ordination, but they misunderstand her stated desire to be a priest. Thérèse makes it clear that she fulfills her desire to be a priest through her unity in the body of Christ with her brothers who are priests. Through them her own priesthood is fulfilled and through the missionary priests her desire to be a missionary is fulfilled. Thérèse writes, "Jesus granted me the favour I desired, he united me in the bonds of the spirit to two of his apostles who became my brothers."[26] When the prioress asked her to write to and pray for the missionary priest Father Adolphe Roulland, she says, "Mother, I did not know how to express my happiness."[27] At the heart of Thérèse's desire to be a missionary is the wish to embrace the whole of humanity. Like the most fervent Evangelical she wants to "win souls for Jesus." She says to her sister, "Oh my Céline, let us live for souls, let us be apostles";[28] and she reaches out to fulfill her calling through her life of sacrifice and prayer.

Thus Thérèse's missionary vocation is fulfilled most of all in the depths of her own contemplative vocation. She has no time for the idea that contemplation is separate from action. For her, as Balthasar points out, contemplation *is* action; Mary and Martha are one. Thérèse is not a passive person. "A soul that is burning with love cannot remain inactive,"[29] she writes. One witness reported, "Sister Thérèse of the Child Jesus had an extremely active and energetic soul beneath her gentle and friendly appearance. Her actions at all times bore the marks of a very strong character and a manly spirit."[30] As a willed decision Thérèse embraced the whole human race through the action of contemplative Love.

> The religious life seemed to her primarily a means of saving souls. She even thought at one time of becoming a nun in the foreign missions; but the hope of being able to save more souls by penance and sacrifice was responsible for her decision to enclose herself in Carmel.[31]

Thérèse thinks of contemplation as the ultimate source of fruitfulness, "the most powerful active force in the Church and the most helpful for sinners."[32]

She believes her contemplative vocation makes her the "mother of souls"[33] and regards the contemplative life as the driving force and energy of the Church's mission. She writes about her vocation to redeem all things in Christ:

> Our vocation . . . is not to go harvesting in the fields of ripe corn; Jesus does not say to us, 'Lower your eyes, look at the fields and go and reap them'; our mission is still loftier. Here are Jesus' words, 'Lift up your eyes and see. . . .' Is not the apostolate of prayer lifted higher, so to speak, than the apostolate of preaching? Our mission as Carmelites is to form to those gospel laborers, they will save millions of souls whose mothers we shall be![34]

Her desire to embrace everyone and everything extends to her desire for martyrdom. Her contemplative mission relies on suffering to complete its full identification with Christ. Just as she desires "all" when it comes to the different vocations in the Church, she also wants all when it comes to martyrdom.

> I cannot confine myself to desiring one kind of martyrdom. To satisfy me I need *all.* Like You, my Adorable Spouse, I would be scourged and crucified. I would die flayed like St. Bartholomew, I would be plunged into boiling oil like St. John; I would undergo all the tortures inflicted upon the martyrs. With St. Agnes and St. Cecilia, I would present my neck to the sword and like Joan of Arc, my dear sister, I would whisper at the stake Your Name, O JESUS. . . . Jesus, if I wanted to write all my desires, I would have to borrow Your Book of Life, for in it are reported all the actions of all the saints and I would accomplish them all for You![35]

It is in her reading of 1 Corinthians 13 that her desire for "all" is consummated. "I understood that Love comprised all vocations, that love was everything, that it embraced all times and places, in a word that it was eternal! . . . I shall be Love. Thus I shall be everything, and thus my dream shall be realised."[36] By claiming a share in universal Love Thérèse claims all things. She does this by virtue of her spiritual childhood.

> I would be afraid to find myself overwhelmed under the weight of my bold desires. My excuse is that I am a child, and children do not reflect on the meaning of their words; however, their parents, once they are placed upon a throne and possess immense treasures, do not hesitate to satisfy the desires of the little ones whom they love as much as they love themselves.[37]

The final paradox for Thérèse is that to be all she must be nothing. Echoing St. John of the Cross, to give light she must be consumed by the dark; she must die so she may live. "In order that Love be fully satisfied, it is necessary that It lower Itself, and that It lower Itself to nothingness and transform this nothingness into fire."[38] Her willingness to offer her life as a sacrifice is the action that grants her all things, for in becoming one with Christ's suffering she also shares in his resurrection of the whole dying world. At this point her tiny life becomes cosmic in its significance. She proves once and for all that the littlest is the best. Thérèse once said, "If the angels were to sweep heaven the dust would be made of diamonds!"[39] In her total humility Thérèse herself is the dust of heaven. Like a tiny morsel of carbon she is crushed by eternal Love and transformed into an immortal diamond. Out of this transformation she rises to reflect the glory of the Lord and shine like a star in the universe.[40] Out of this sacrifice she promises, "I will come down,"[41] and she sees that she will "spend her heaven doing good on earth."[42]

Some forfeit their souls to gain the physical world; Thérèse forfeits herself to gain the whole universe. She can only ask for "all" because she is prepared to give all. She knows God answers prayer, so she asks boldly for the fullness of his grace. Balthasar points out the stupendous desire of this twenty-four-year-old girl:

> Other saints are content with their place in the order of the Church; Thérèse says, 'I shall be everything.' Thérèse is not to be localised. She will be everywhere and nowhere. She wishes to make herself felt throughout the whole house, like the aroma of Christ; she will be — and this is perhaps her shrewdest description of herself — a light, a ray issuing from the brow of her Mother, the Church.[43]

He goes on to quote Thérèse's triumphant words: "Now, then, I am a child of the Church and the Church is a Queen since she is Your Bride, O divine King of Kings! The heart of a little child does not seek riches and glory. She understands that this glory belongs by right to her brothers, the angels and saints. Her own glory will be the reflected glory shining from her Mother's forehead."[44]

In embracing all things, Thérèse expands the Benedictine vows beyond the personal. In her total obedience, she calls the whole world to obey God's created order and find peace in His will. This submission to the divine will replaces war with peace, anarchy with order, and chaos with harmony. New life springs out of this new order. In Thérèse's expanded vision, conversion of life means not just the conversion of an individual life, or the conversion of many lives, but the conversion of every atom and galaxy, of Life itself. St. Paul said the "whole world was groaning for redemption"; with him Thérèse sees the result of Christ's work, and her own prayers as being nothing less than the redemption of the whole world.

Thérèse's embrace of all things connects with the same mystical unity that Benedict experienced that night when "the whole world was gathered up before his eyes in what appeared to be a single ray of light."[45] That Thérèse and Benedict received "all" is a sign that we can share in their glory. Benedict gives us an ordinary way, and Thérèse insists that all Christians can follow her little way of spiritual childhood if they will. Thérèse proves that within the most ordinary of lives contemplation is possible; prayer is possible; the sacrifice of self is possible; and a participation in the redemption of the world is possible. Thérèse accomplished this mission in and through the Church, and she insists to the end that God does the work: "It is to God alone that all value must be attributed; there's nothing of value in my little nothingness."[46] To enter into the ordinary life of grace with Thérèse is to seek small sacrifices, to remain hidden, trusting as a little child in God's goodness. As we grow into this extraordinary life, within the ordinary we will begin to experience with Thérèse the agony and the ecstasy of sharing in the new birth of the old world. This means claiming our share in God's creation, a share that is not less than everything. As St. Paul wrote to the Christians at Corinth, "Whether . . . the world or life or death or the present or the future, all are yours; and you are Christ's; and Christ is God's."[47] Thérèse realizes the final secret is that to embrace all things is to be embraced by the God who made them. Throughout her writings Thérèse embraced "all" through her confidence that "underneath are the everlasting arms."[48]

In the final words of her manuscript, written in a spidery, weakened hand, Thérèse expresses her simple desire to run into

God's embrace: "Yes, I feel it! even though I had on my conscience all the sins that can be committed, I would go . . . and
throw myself in Jesus' arms. . . . I go to him with confidence and
love."[49]

Chapter Nine Endnotes

1. Vita Sackville-West, *The Eagle and the Dove, A Study in Contrasts,*
London, Michael Joseph, 1943, p. 164.
2. Ibid., p. 165.
3. Ibid.
4. Ibid., p. 167.
5. Thomas N. Taylor (tr.), *Saint Thérèse of Lisieux, The Little Flower of
Jesus,* New York, P. J. Kenedy, 1926, pp. 267-268.
6. Hans Urs Von Balthasar, *Two Sisters in the Spirit,* San Francisco,
Ignatius Press, 1970, p. 25.
7. Ibid., p. 29.
8. Ibid.
9. John Clarke, O.C.D. (tr.), *St. Thérèse of Lisieux: Her Last Conversations,* Washington, D.C., ICS Publications, 1977, p. 103.
10. Ibid., p. 126.
11. Ibid.
12. Ibid., p. 102.
13. John Clarke, O.C.D. (tr.), *The Story of a Soul: The Autobiography of
St. Thérèse of Lisieux,* Washington, D.C., ICS Publications, 1976, pp. 253-
254.
14. Balthasar, p. 30.
15. Quoted in Clarke, *[St. Thérèse's] Last Conversations,* p. 10.
16. Clarke, *The Story of a Soul,* p. 27.
17. Ibid., p. 37.
18. Ibid., p. 125.
19. Ibid., pp. 125-126.
20. Ibid.
21. Ibid., pp. 139-140.
22. Ibid., p. 192.
23. Ibid., p. 253.
24. Ibid., pp. 192-193.

25. John Clarke, O.C.D. (tr.), *General Correspondence, Vol. II*, Washington, D.C., ICS Publications, 1988, p. 1095.
26. Clarke, *The Story of a Soul*, pp. 250-251.
27. Ibid.
28. Clarke, *General Correspondence, Vol. I*, p. 578.
29. Clarke, *The Story of a Soul*, p. 257.
30. H. Petitot, O.P., *Saint Thérèse de Lisieux: Une Renaissance spirituelle*, Paris, Desclée, 1925, p. 125.
31. Ibid., p. 126.
32. Balthasar, p. 194.
33. Clarke, *The Story of a Soul*, p. 192.
34. Clarke, *General Correspondence, Vol. II*, p. 753.
35. Clarke, *The Story of a Soul*, p. 193.
36. Ibid., p. 194.
37. Ibid., p. 196.
38. Ibid., p. 195.
39. Clarke, *[St. Thérèse's] Last Conversations*, p. 106.
40. Cf. 2 Corinthians 3:18 and Philippians 2:15.
41. Clarke, *[St. Thérèse's] Last Conversations*, p. 228.
42. Ibid., p. 102.
43. Balthasar, p. 210.
44. Clarke, *The Story of a Soul*, p. 196.
45. Odo Zimmerman, O.S.B., and Benedict Avery, O.S.B. (tr.), *Life and Miracles of St. Benedict* (Book II of the *Dialogues*), Prologue, Collegeville, Minnesota, The Liturgical Press, 1987, p. 35.
46. Clarke, *[St. Thérèse's] Last Conversations*, p. 141.
47. 1 Corinthians 3:22-23.
48. Cf. Deuteronomy 33:27.
49. Clarke, *The Story of a Soul*, p. 259.

Ten

The Porter's Perfection

Thoughts and Prayers

There is no fear in love, but perfect love casts out fear. For fear has to do with punishment, and he who fears is not perfected in love.

— 1 John 4:18

And above all these put on love, which binds everything together in perfect harmony.

— Colossians 3:14

The abundance of His love
will do more to correct you
than all your anxious self-contemplation.

— Fénelon

Love cannot be taught.

— St. Basil

Love holds the world together, and if we could forget ourselves everything in the world would fly into a perfect harmony.

— Iris Murdoch

Love bade me welcome.

— George Herbert

Prayer

Lord God, set me free from all evil passions that I may be made fit to love. Nothing is sweeter than love, nothing more courageous, nothing fuller nor better in heaven and earth. So let me love you more than myself, nor love myself but for you, and in you all that truly love you.

— Thomas à Kempis

Finding a holy man is like trying to find buried treasure without a map. Like the quest to discover the Holy Grail, finding a holy man is full of pitfalls, illusion, and paradox. It is natural to begin the search by turning to those who advertise. But those who advertise their holiness are not humble, and therefore not holy. Every self-promoting guru, preacher, teacher, priest, or prophet is pushing his personality, not his perfection. If we turn to a respectable religious person, we may be equally disappointed because it is easy to mistake good manners for holiness of life. A charismatic leader, an eloquent speaker, or a compassionate counselor may offer help, but he will not necessarily offer holiness. Furthermore, it is often among the professional religious people that the brood of vipers called Pharisees lurks. We might start by being smitten and end up being bitten. To complicate the quest further, if we should find a person we think is holy, he will tell us most assuredly that he is *not* holy. Such a person will either chuckle with glee at our mistake or tell us to go away.

The holy person is a hidden person. It is true that God raises up some saints to be heroic, but beneath their heroic accomplishments lies a soul that is hidden in an ordinary life. Thérèse says:

> One must consent to stay always poor and without strength, and that's the difficulty, for where are we to find the man truly poor in spirit? He must be sought afar, says the psalmist. He does not say we must look for him among great souls, but 'afar,' that is in lowliness, nothingness. Let us stay very far from all that is brilliant.[1]

If this is so, then the saint is difficult to find. She is treasure buried in a field, a lost coin, and a pearl of great price hidden in an oyster bed at the bottom of the sea.

If the greatest saints are truly hidden, then it could be that there are far more of them than anyone reckons. They are hidden in this world now, but in heaven these nobodies will be the celebrities. In his colorful story about purgatory, C. S. Lewis shows such an ordinary saint in her full glory:

> There was a procession . . . first came bright Spirits . . . then, on the left and right, at each side of the forest avenue, came youthful shapes, boys upon one hand, and girls upon the other. If I could remember their singing and write down the notes, no man who read that score would ever grow sick or old. Between them went musicians: and after these a lady in whose honour all this was being done. . . . I remember the unbearable beauty of her face. . . .
> 'Is it? . . . Is it?' I whispered to my guide.
> 'Not at all,' said he. 'It's someone you'll never have heard of. Her name on earth was Sarah Smith and she lived at Golders Green. . . .' 'She is one of the great ones. . . . You have heard that fame in this country and fame on Earth are two quite different things.'[2]

The greatest of saints may be Sarah Smith, who lives over the chip shop in Golders Green; or perhaps Jim Allen, who sells work shoes to farmers; or maybe even Laura Keen, who brings up five children to love and serve the Lord. In the economy of eternity it is these hidden ones who accomplish the most. So Thérèse observes:

> Very often without our knowing it, the graces and lights we receive are due to a hidden soul, for God wills that the saints communicate grace to each other through prayer with great love . . . how often have I thought that I may

owe all the graces I've received to the prayers of a person who begged them from God for me and whom I shall know only in heaven.[3]

Elsewhere she imagines the friendships in heaven between the great saints and the little souls:

> Do you not think that on their side the great saints, seeing what they owe to quite little souls, will love them with an incomparable love? Delightful and surprising will be the friendships found there — I am sure of it. The favoured companion of an Apostle or a great Doctor of the Church will perhaps be a young shepherd lad; and a simple little child may be the intimate friend of a patriarch.[4]

That the saint may be an ordinary person, indeed must be an ordinary person, is both encouraging and terrifying. It is encouraging for all those who are simple and pure of heart. But for anyone who is the slightest bit extraordinary the fact that holiness is ordinary causes dismay. Thérèse says we must "stay very far from anything that is brilliant," but if one is brilliant by virtue of talent, intelligence, privilege, and education, then the idea that salvation lies hidden in the ordinary life becomes an alarming proposition. After all, it seems "some men are born great, some achieve greatness, and some have greatness thrust upon them." If one is extraordinary through no fault of one's own, then it is disconcerting to find that salvation seems beyond one's reach.

Søren Kierkegaard recognized this in his extended meditation on the man of faith. In *Fear and Trembling* he says he had looked long and hard for the man of faith, then realized that the man of faith is a simple, ordinary fellow. "But he looks like a tax collector!"[5] Kierkegaard exclaims. He lives a contented and unremarkable life. He goes to work, goes to church, loves and serves his family, and is completely hidden in humility. The man of faith is natural. He lives in perfect harmony with his Creator. Because he is as he should be, he does not appear remarkable. It is only the unnatural that is unusual. Flying pigs surprise us; flying parrots don't. Confronted with this ordinary man of faith, Kierkegaard, who is a poet and philosopher, despairs. As a thinker he is an extraordinary person and he can't help it. He knows too much. He analyzes too much. He thinks about himself too much to be a man of faith. Simply by the fact that he recognizes the man of faith, Kierkegaard concludes he can never be one. This is the cruel irony, and this is why Thérèse says that "one must consent to stay without strength, and that's the difficulty."[6]

Both the privileged and the poor, the brilliant and the dull, may be ordinary if they can cease to be self-conscious; and the worst form of self-consciousness is self-analysis. What cripples Kierkegaard is the depth of his self-analytical nature. The analytical soul is always checking to see if he has "arrived," when nine times out of ten he hasn't yet determined the proper destination. Self-analysis is dangerous because we can't be objective about the state of our mind and soul. We are both too hard and too easy on ourselves. Insecurity pushes us to indulge in the form of self-pity called "a poor self-image" while the same insecurity causes us to be arrogant, bossy, and proud.

In fact, spiritual self-judgment is not just dangerous, it is impossible. We are told to know ourselves, but this is humanistic common sense — the sort of common sense that is commonly nonsense. Without God's grace, how can I really know myself? How can I begin to understand the labyrinths of the mind, the caverns of the soul, and the terrifying realm of the unconscious? The maze of motives, desires, and circumstances is too complex for anyone, least of all myself, to ever solve. Isn't it obvious that the one person who will forever be a mystery to me is me?

Thérèse was well aware that spiritual judgment was impossible:

> If the devil tries to point out to me the defects of such and such a Sister who is less attractive to me, I immediately hasten to discover her virtues and good motive; I say to myself that, if I have seen her fall once, she may well have gained many victories over herself that she is hiding out of humility; and that even what appears to me a fault may really be an act of virtue on account of its intention . . . this little experience I had showed me we must never judge . . . since my small acts of virtue can be mistaken for imperfections, it is just as possible for people to be mistaken in taking for virtue what is nothing but imperfection.[7]

Thérèse echoes St. Paul, who also wrote about the impossibility of judging ourselves: "Indeed I do not even judge myself. My conscience is clear, but that does not make me innocent. It is the Lord who judges me. Therefore judge nothing before the appointed time; wait until the Lord comes, he will bring to light what is hidden in darkness and will expose the motives of men's hearts."[8]

Thérèse recognizes that the pure of heart don't bother with final judgment, not because they are trying hard to bite their tongue, but because they don't see the problem: "To the pure, all things are pure . . . a simple, modest soul sees evil in nothing."[9] In her final months she says, "I always see the good side of things. Some people take everything the way that will cause them the most trouble. With me it is the opposite. Even when I have nothing but suffering . . . well, I make this my joy."[10]

"He who knows all forgives all," goes the old saying. Therefore judgment of ourselves or others is unfair because we don't have all the facts. Judgment is also biased because it is usually driven by a foregone conclusion. When we judge others, we have already decided to condemn them. When we judge ourselves, we have probably already decided to be lenient, and if we are not too lenient on ourselves, then we are too harsh. Benedict helps his monks to avoid pointless judgment with both kind words and stern words: the brothers should, "with the greatest patience make allowance for one another's weaknesses whether physical or moral."[11] But concerning oneself: "Whenever one perceives any good in oneself to attribute it to God, not to one's self, but to recognise that whatever is evil is one's own doing and to blame one's self and to fear the Day of Judgement."[12] Benedict's other cure for self-analysis is the habit of obedience. One should "obey the Abbot's commands in everything."[13] Obedience eviscerates self-analysis. Suddenly there is only one question to ask oneself, and the Sunday school song has the answer, "Trust and obey, for there's no other way to be happy in Jesus but to trust and obey." Therefore all one can say is "I trusted and obeyed" or "I failed to trust and obey." All other judgments must be left to the Eternal Judge.

Since self-judgment is impossible, awareness of spiritual progress is also impossible. A sudden and terrifying truth dawns on us that we really cannot know if we are getting anywhere at all. The realization that progress is unrecognizable leaves us suspended on the "edge of the grimpen [a marshy area] where there is no secure foothold."[14] The final paradox is even more disconcerting: the realization dawns that for a soul not to be aware of progress is almost a guarantee of progress. In other words, when

Thérèse writes, "I will be tormented by a foolish thing I said or did, then I turn to myself and say, Ah, still standing at the same spot as at the beginning!"[15] she is giving evidence that humility is present, and if she is becoming genuinely humble, then she has made progress after all. Thérèse is well aware of the paradox and tells us: "Now I have reconciled myself to seeing myself imperfect always and even to finding my joy in it. . . . I learned very quickly that the farther one advances along this road, the farther from the goal one believes oneself to be."[16]

When the full import of this paradox is considered, it becomes so hot that only the coolly pure of heart can handle it. If no progress is the only guarantee of progress, then any imperfect soul might mistake complacency or even mortal sin for sanctity. In a moment I could fall over the edge, like the character of Graham Greene's who thought his loss of faith was the dark night of the soul. If I fall into the error of mistaking my complacency for great sanctity, I may confound it by imagining that I am also humble, and therefore a very great saint indeed.

Spiritual self-analysis is like walking a tightrope while blindfolded and wearing lead boots. Once its utter impossibility dawns on us, we are hit with the reality that there is only one thing we can know for certain about ourselves: that we are sinners. This is why one of the most ancient and existential prayers is the prayer of the heart in which we simply repeat at the core of our being, "Lord Jesus Christ, Son of God, have mercy on me, a sinner." The awareness of our basic alienation from God means we are constantly conscious of our desperate emptiness. Our sole success in the spiritual quest is the acute awareness of our failure. So, when an old monk was asked what the monks do in the monastery, he said, "We fall and get up again, then fall and get up again." Likewise, Thérèse writes, "Look at little children; they are always breaking things, tearing things, falling down while loving their parents very much."[17]

If our status as sinners is the one thing we can know about ourselves, the one certain thing we can know about God is that his grace is all. This is the knowledge that leads us to true self-awareness. Two things are eternally true: I am a sinner and God's goodness sustains me. Thérèse instructs one of her novices that her stumbling is a falling into humility and trust in God's grace:

> If God wants you to be as weak and powerless as a child . . . resign yourself, then, to stumbling at every step. To falling even. Love your powerlessness and your soul will benefit more from it than if, aided by grace, you were to behave with enthusiastic heroism and fill your soul with self satisfaction and pride.[18]

Once more Thérèse echoes St. Paul who recounts the Lord's words, "My grace is enough for you: my power is made perfect in weakness." He goes on to say, "I will all the more gladly boast of my weaknesses, that the power of Christ may rest upon me. For the sake of Christ, then, I am content with weaknesses, . . . for when I am weak, then I am strong."[19]

Benedict says his little Rule for beginners can "bring them to the heights of learning and virtue,"[20] but on first reading he does not seem to give an example of what the perfect monk looks like. The abbot is a wise father in God, but not necessarily the perfect monk. The cellarer is also a wise and loving father, but he doesn't necessarily exhibit the traits of the perfect monk. Instead, in a touch that Thérèse would have loved, Benedict hides the perfect monk in a little chapter about a most humble officer of the monastery. Scholars think chapter sixty-four may well have been the original end of the Rule. If so, then at the end of

his Rule Benedict shows us the perfect monk. This is where the
Rule brings us: to a little person with a lowly job — he is the old
doorkeeper of the monastery.

> At the gate of the monastery a wise old man is to be
> posted, one capable of receiving a message and giving a
> reply and whose maturity guarantees that he will not wan-
> der around. This doorkeeper should have a cell near the
> gate, so that persons who arrive may always find someone
> at hand to give them a reply.[21]

This old monk is content doing one of the humblest jobs
in the community. He maintains the contemplative life, but
his cell is near the door, looking outward to the needy world.
That he does not wander shows that he has mastered his vow
of stability. His obedience has become natural, for he serves
not only the abbot who has placed him in such a lowly position, but to all who come to the monastery. "As soon as anyone
knocks, or a poor man calls out . . . with all the gentleness that
comes from the fear of God, he should speedily and with the
warmth of charity attend to the enquirer."[22] The old porter
remembers that Christ is present in every guest and so to each
knock on the door he calls out, "Thanks be to God," or "God
bless you!"[23] In his childlike simplicity the porter is almost comic
— like one of those old fools in Shakespeare who speaks the
truth in the midst of his master's foolishness. Benedict doesn't
say so, but perhaps the old man was once a prior or even an
abbot, but now as the lowly porter he is the embodiment of the
Benedictine ideal. His life is fulfilled in hidden humility and
perfect love.

Perfect Love is that state when a person has come to the
"condition of complete simplicity costing not less than every-

thing."[24] Benedict's old porter is simple. He has relearned the innocent dependence of the young child, and becoming as a little child he has already entered God's kingdom. Benedict teaches that Perfect Love can only be approached through a lifetime of grace-empowered obedience. At the end of his chapter on humility he describes the state of living in Perfect Love:

> Thus when all these steps of humility have been climbed, the monk will soon reach that love of God which, being perfect, drives out all fear. Through this love all the practices which before he kept somewhat fearfully, he now begins to keep effortlessly and naturally and habitually, influenced now not by any fear of hell, but by the force of long practice, and the very delight he experiences in virtue. These things the Lord, working through his Holy Spirit, will deign to show in his workman, when he has been thus purified from vice and sin.[25]

In the old porter Benedict shows us a soul who has learned to live in the simplicity of pure obedience and perfect love.

Pure obedience and love are facets of the same jewel. To love another person is to desire the very best for that individual; to obey is to sacrifice oneself for the sake of the beloved, therefore obedience and love are one. When love is perfect, the simple soul is not even aware of the obedience she is practicing. Thérèse says, "True glory is that which will last eternally and to reach it, it isn't necessary to perform striking works but to hide oneself and practice virtue in such a way that the left hand does not know what the right hand is doing."[26]

Without love, obedience is worthless slavery; but when obedience and love are one, there is absolute freedom. Absolute freedom means absolute power so that together obedience and love can overcome the power of fear. Thérèse says, "I regard it as a real grace that I have been accustomed since my childhood to overcome fear,"[27] and Balthasar observes, "Thérèse learns that one can do things out of love and obedience that, in themselves, and apart from love, would fill one with fear, but perfect love drives out fear."[28]

Perfect Love is the perfection of the ordinary. The simple soul, like Benedict's porter or countless other hidden saints, lives in a state of simplicity that is unremarkable because it is natural. This is the "tax clerk" who troubles Kierkegaard's agonized soul. This is Thérèse, hidden in her convent in a provincial French town. This is Benedict, scraping a living out of the soil of Italy with his brothers. These souls are not hidden because they are scurrying for cover. They are hidden because they have finally fit into their place in the universe and therefore no longer stick out. If this obscurity is a sign of sanctity, then it should be seen most of all in the Gospel.

In the life of Christ it explains the riddle of the "Messianic Secret" in the Gospel of Mark. Why did Jesus order people not to report his miracles and to keep quiet about his identity? For the same reason that he was constantly slipping away to a secret mountaintop to pray. At the heart of his public ministry was a private soul. At the heart of his heroic life was a hidden life of prayer, and like every saint he wanted most of all to remain unknown. When he prayed for the cup to be taken from him, his own most fervent desire may have been to return to the calm monotony of the carpenter's shop in Nazareth, where he enjoyed a unity with his father that was hidden in an ordinary life.

This obscurity is also evident in the life of his mother. The Blessed Virgin Mary exemplifies the hidden perfection God has in store for all Christians. Someone may logically ask why Mary was not recognized immediately as the first and greatest saint, but this is to miss the nature of sanctity. Mary was little. She was a young girl when the angel came to her, and she kept that innocent simplicity throughout her life. She was hidden in Nazareth and troubled by the supernatural intervention in her life.[29] Mary was filled with God's grace, but that plenitude did not make her into a superhuman creature like some fairy godmother. Instead the grace in Mary's life perfected her natural humanity.

If anyone were to meet Mary, that person might be aware of a calm confidence lacking in other women. If such individuals were sensitive, they might have glimpsed some unusual depth of peace. They might have heard the joy of heaven in her laughter and caught a glint of eternity in her eyes, but to most people she seemed an ordinary woman. She seemed ordinary because she was perfect, and "perfect" means whole or complete. She was simply who she was created to be, and when things are as natural they are not unusual. When the ancient theologians said Mary was the second Eve, they did not mean she was some sort of mother goddess. They meant Mary was Woman with her first-created innocence and simplicity restored. Mary was natural as Eve was natural, and as a result she was both as wonderful and as ordinary as a day in May.

Thérèse understood this extraordinary ordinariness of Mary: "What does me a lot of good when I think of the Holy Family is to imagine a life that was very ordinary . . . their life was the same as ours."[30] She has no time for pious platitudes about the Virgin Mary.

All the sermons on Mary I have heard have left me cold. How I should love to have been a priest in order to preach about the Mother of God! . . . I would begin by showing how the life of the Mother of God is, in fact, very little known. . . . It is surely easy to sense that her life in Nazareth and later must have been perfectly ordinary.[31]

Thérèse also recognizes the reason for Mary's perfect ordinariness: "The unique privilege of Mary is that she remained free from original sin."[32] Like all Truth, this dogmatic Truth is also a practical Truth. It points us from what we are to what we shall be. By God's grace Mary was kept in a state of perfect love, and this condition of complete simplicity is what all of us are called to. Jesus himself calls us to this perfection, saying, "You, therefore, must be perfect, as your heavenly Father is perfect."[33] James writes, "Perseverance must finish its work in you so that you may be perfect and complete, not lacking anything."[34] The same grace that was at work in Mary's life God is constantly willing and working to bring us to the same innocent perfection she enjoyed. He wants us to drop all judgment and self-analysis to live in the fullness of who we are.

To live in a state of perfect love requires submission to God's recreative power in our lives. We may fall, but we get up again. We do not sin, so that grace may abound, but for the one who lives in perfect love, every imperfection is only a spur that drives us further into God's care. We begin this work by taking up the tools of perfection that Father Benedict offers. As his child we must promise "before God and all his saints . . . stability, conversion of life and obedience."[35] Then in time, no matter what our age, we may come to live like the old porter in a state of mature innocence.

Living in this perfect love is the end of the little way of St. Benedict. It is summed up in the childlike words of Thérèse, who whispers from her terrible deathbed: "Sanctity does not consist in performing such and such acts; it means being ready at heart to become small and humble in the arms of God, acknowledging our weakness and trusting in his fatherly goodness to the point of audacity."[36]

Chapter Ten Endnotes

1. F. J. Sheed (tr.), *Collected Letters of St. Thérèse of Lisieux*, London, Sheed and Ward, 1989, p. 253.
2. C. S. Lewis, *The Great Divorce*, Glasgow, HarperCollins, 1988, pp. 97-98.
3. John Clarke, O.C.D. (tr.), *St. Thérèse of Lisieux: Her Last Conversations*, Washington, D.C., ICS Publications, 1977, pp. 99-100.
4. Thomas N. Taylor (tr.), *Saint Thérèse of Lisieux, The Little Flower of Jesus*, New York, P. J. Kenedy, 1926, p. 302.
5. Søren Kierkegaard, *Fear and Trembling*, Princeton University Press, 1945, p. 53.
6. Sheed, p. 253.
7. John Clarke, O.C.D. (tr.), *The Story of a Soul: The Autobiography of St. Thérèse of Lisieux*, Washington, D.C., ICS Publications, 1976, pp. 221-222.
8. 1 Corinthians 4:4-5.
9. Clarke, *The Story of a Soul*, p. 123.
10. Clarke, *[St. Thérèse's] Last Conversations*, p. 51.
11. Abbot Parry (tr.), *The Rule of St. Benedict*, Leominster, Gracewing, 1999, p. 116.
12. Parry, p. 18.
13. Ibid., p. 19.
14. T. S. Eliot, *The Four Quartets*, London, Faber and Faber, 1986, p. 23.
15. Clarke, *[St. Thérèse's] Last Conversations*, pp. 73-74.
16. Clarke, *The Story of a Soul*, p. 158.
17. Clarke, *[St. Thérèse's] Last Conversations*, p. 140.
18. Sheed, p. 250.
19. 2 Corinthians 12:9-10.
20. Parry, p. 118.
21. Ibid., p. 107.
22. Ibid.
23. Ibid.
24. T. S. Eliot, *The Four Quartets*, p. 48.
25. Parry, p. 29.
26. Clarke, *The Story of a Soul*, p. 72.
27. Ibid., p. 43.
28. Hans Urs Von Balthasar, *Two Sisters in the Spirit*, San Francisco, Ignatius Press, 1970, p. 132.

29. Cf. Luke 2:29.
30. Clarke, *[St. Thérèse's] Last Conversations*, p. 159.
31. Ibid., p. 161.
32. Ibid., p. 162.
33. Matthew 5:48.
34. James 1:4.
35. Parry, p. 94.
36. Clarke, *[St. Thérèse's] Last Conversations*, p. 129.

Bibliography

(The literature on both Thérèse and Benedict is vast. This selected bibliography includes the books the author has found most helpful.)

Balthasar, Hans Urs Von. *Two Sisters in the Spirit*. San Francisco: Ignatius Press, 1970.

Cary-Elwes, Columba, O.S.B. *Work and Prayer, the Rule of St. Benedict for Lay People*. Tunbridge Wells: Burns and Oates, 1992.

Cassian, John. *Conferences*, in Edgar C. S. Gibson (tr.). *Nicene and Post-Nicene Fathers*, Grand Rapids, Mich.: William Eerdmans, 1964.

Chesterton, G. K. *St. Thomas Aquinas*. London: Hodder and Stoughton, 1943.

Chittister, Joan. *The Rule of Benedict — Insight for the Ages*. New York: Crossroad, 1998.

Clarke, John, O.C.D. (tr.). *General Correspondence, Vol. I*. Washington, D.C.: ICS Publications, 1988.

――――. *General Correspondence, Vol. II*. Washington, D.C.: ICS Publications, 1988.

――――. *St. Thérèse of Lisieux: Her Last Conversations*. Washington, D.C.: ICS Publications, 1977.

――――. *The Story of a Soul: The Autobiography of St. Thérèse of Lisieux*. Washington, D.C.: ICS Publications, 1976.

de Waal, Esther. *Seeking God*. London: Fount Paperbacks, 1988.

――――. *A Life-Giving Way*. Collegeville, Minn.: Liturgical Press, 1995.

Dostoyevsky, Fyodor. *The Brothers Karamazov*. New York: Random House, 1950.

Eliot, T. S. *The Four Quartets*. London: Faber and Faber, 1986.

Görres, I. F. *The Hidden Face: A Study of St. Thérèse of Lisieux*. London: Burns and Oates, 1959.

Hart, Patrick and Montaldo, Jonathan (eds.). *The Intimate Merton*. Oxford: Lion, 1999.

Hooper, Walter and Lancelyn Green, Roger. *C. S. Lewis — A Biography*. London: Collins, 1974.

Hopkins, Gerard Manley. "God's Grandeur," in *The Faber Book of Religious Verse*. Helen Gardner (ed.). London: Faber and Faber, 1972.

An Irish Carmelite (tr.). *Thoughts of Saint Therese.* Rockford, Ill.: Tan Books, 1915.

Kierkegaard, Søren. *Fear and Trembling.* Princeton University Press, 1945.

Knox, Ronald (tr.). *Autobiography of a Saint.* London: Collins, 1973.

Le Joly, E., S.J. *We Do It For Jesus — Mother Teresa.* London: Darton, Longman and Todd, 1977.

Lewis, C. S. *The Great Divorce.* Glasgow: HarperCollins, 1988.

_____. *Mere Christianity.* London: HarperCollins, 1995.

_____. *Miracles.* London: Fount, 1978.

Longenecker, Dwight. *Listen My Son.* Leominster: Gracewing, 2000.

Merton, Thomas. *Conjectures of a Guilty Bystander.* New York: Doubleday, 1966.

_____. *The Seven Storey Mountain.* London: SPCK, 1961.

_____. *The Wisdom of the Desert.* London: Sheldon Press, 1960.

Mork, Wulstan, O.S.B. *The Benedictine Way.* Petersham: St. Bede's Publications, 1987.

Nelson, John. *Living the Little Way of Love.* London: New City, 1999.

Nichols, Aidan, O.P. *Christendom Awake.* Edinburgh: T&T Clark, 1999.

Nouwen, Henri J. M. *The Genesee Diary: Report from a Trappist Monastery.* New York: Doubleday, 1976.

Parry, Abbot (tr.). *The Rule of St. Benedict.* Leominster: Gracewing, 1997.

Petitot, H., O.P. *Saint Thérèse de Lisieux: Une Renaissance spirituelle.* Paris: Desclée, 1925.

Rees, Daniel, O.S.B. *Consider Your Call — A Theology of the Monastic Life Today.* London: SPCK, 1978.

Sackville-West, Vita. *The Eagle and the Dove, A Study in Contrasts.* London: Michael Joseph, 1943.

Saward, John. *The Way of the Lamb.* Edinburgh: T&T Clark, 1999.

Sayers, Dorothy L. and Reynolds, Barbara (trs.). *Paradiso.* London: Penguin, 1976.

Sheed, F. J. (tr.). *Collected Letters of Saint Thérèse of Lisieux.* London: Sheed and Ward, 1949.

Stead, Julian, O.S.B. *Saint Benedict — A Rule for Beginners.* New York: New City, 1994.

Stewart, Columba, O.S.B. *Prayer and Community.* London: Darton, Longman and Todd, 1998.

Suzuki, Shunryu. *Zen Mind, Beginner's Mind.* T. Dixon (ed.). New York: Weatherill, 1970.

Taylor, Thomas N. (tr.). *Saint Thérèse of Lisieux, The Little Flower of Jesus.* New York: P. J. Kenedy, 1926.

Traherne, Thomas. *Centuries of Meditations*. London: Faith Press, 1964.
Vaughn, Henry. "The Revival," in *The Faber Book of Religious Verse*. Helen
   Gardner (ed.). London: Faber and Faber, 1972.
_____. "The World," in *The Faber Book of Religious Verse*. Helen Gardner
   (ed.). London: Faber and Faber, 1972.
Wolter, Maurus, O.S.B. *The Principles of Monasticism*. St. Louis: Herder
   Book Co., 1962.
Zimmerman, Odo, O.S.B. and Avery, Benedict, O.S.B. (trs.). *Life and
   Miracles of St. Benedict* (Book II of the *Dialogues*). Collegeville, Minn.:
   The Liturgical Press, 1987.

Lightning Source UK Ltd.
Milton Keynes UK
UKOW04f2207080315

247520UK00001B/6/P